ESCAPE FROM THE KITCHEN

ESCAPE FROM THE KITCHEN

Deniece Schofield

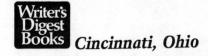 Cincinnati, Ohio

Library of Congress Cataloging-in-Publication Data

Schofield, Deniece, 1947-
   Escape from the kitchen.

   Includes index.
   1. Kitchens. 2. Cookery. 3. House cleaning. I. Title.
TX653.S36 1986   648   86-15985
ISBN 0-89879-231-2

Design by Joan Ann Jacobus

ACKNOWLEDGMENTS

Our five children have spent most of their lives wreaking havoc with our kitchen, providing me with the perfect laboratory in which to test my theories.

My husband, Jim, has Mr. Mom'd his way into my heart forever, giving me the time to test my theories.

And Cincinnati's own Beth Franks, the world's greatest freelance editor, has scraped, rinsed, and scoured this manuscript, putting all my theories in apple pie order.

CONTENTS

Is Closed • The Schedule of Events—Your Cleaning
Schedule • Get It Done! • Family Organizer • Plan-
ning Notebook • Filing System—Appliance Record
• Errand Drawer • Landing/Launch Pads • Tool Box
• Junk Drawer • Phone Cord • Dishes? Toss 'em in
the Trash • Nitty Gritty Notes

—— INTRODUCTION

I am a kitchen expert. My credentials? Well, I can make a pot scrubber out of nylon net (plus 100 other things); I have fourteen recipes that call for Oreo cookies (without the middle); I know thirty-seven methods (count 'em thirty-seven) for peeling onions without shedding a tear; I've arrested the rust in my SOS pad; and I do a mean flower arrangement out of dandelions with ½ inch stems, and clover (the backyard variety).

I received my training at the battlefront. You know, the battlefront—where people throw half-eaten grape Popsicles into the pretty wicker wastebasket that sits on the white carpet. They pour the soggy remains of their Frosted Flakes over the clean dishes air-drying in the sink. (It's an honest mistake—the garbage disposal is on that side.)

At the battlefront fifteen-year-old draft dodgers hyperventilate over a sink full of dishes, considering it (the hyperventilating) a ferocious workout. Old Cub Scout injuries seem to flare up at this point, too. Youngsters take the attitude, "There's no need to dry your hands on a paper towel when you've got armpits." And finally, at the battlefront folks gather around the supper table for (what seems to be) the primary purpose of complaining.

Yes, if you live at the zoo long enough you learn how to feed the animals. So, you see, I *am* an expert.

Aside from conquering the typical on-the-job-training problems like flat meringues, dull green beans, and lumpy gravy, I've authored two books: *Confessions of an Organized Housewife* and *Confessions of a Happily Organized Family*. With the success of those two volumes I now find myself lecturing frequently, conducting workshops, and making media appearances. I wrote *Escape from the Kitchen* because everywhere I go, people express keen interest in this subject. They say things like:

"Our kitchen is the kind of horrible nightmare that makes you wake up in a cold sweat."

"I can spend hours cleaning the kitchen, and two minutes later it looks like the Nabisco factory after Cookie Monster was turned loose."

"My kids won't eat anything unless they've seen it sing, dance, and tell jokes or. TV."

Today, our real challenge is time. Many (though not all) of us consider our time to be more valuable than our money. We are paying for convenience and time-saving devices like never before. With time so precious, we need to look to those areas that currently eat up large amounts of time and do what we can to reduce that consumption. The kitchen is a very conspicuous time-consumer.

In their book, *About Time*, authors Alec Mackenzie and Kay Cronkite Waldo said: "The woman who is concerned about managing her time effectively must choose the kitchen as a primary target for more efficient organization." That, in a nutshell, is the purpose of this book.

I'm going to put heavy emphasis on organizing your kitchen workplaces, your kitchen time, and your meal preparation procedures, and you may think at the outset I'm just requiring that you spend *more* time in your kitchen, not less. That's a common complaint I hear from people before they give these methods a try.

For instance, recently on a TV talk show I was demonstrating how we code puzzles. (I know this isn't a kitchen example, but bear with me because it makes a good point.) Each inlaid puzzle is assigned a number and every piece has that same number written on the back. After the show, the producer thanked me for my appearance and complimented me on my performance. Then she said, "Now, if I just had time to code the puzzles."

I made a passing comment such as: "Time sure is hard to come by, isn't it?" and dropped the matter. I hear that argument all the time and I've decided it's a pretty lame excuse.

One person can code an inlaid puzzle in fifteen to thirty seconds; a big five-hundred piece-er might take two minutes. With five kids doing puzzles, and a three-year-old occasionally dumping and mixing them up we have saved literally hours by not having to investigate each piece to determine its ownership. That is only one isolated example, but the same fact is borne out over and over again: planning and organization save time.

I have taught these escape principles to thousands of people. Here are a few testimonials.

"I was a mess. Thinking there was no hope for me I sank deeper in despair and deeper in the mess, assuming I didn't have time to get things organized. A friend gave me your book and I attended one of your workshops. Now I can see how right you were about saving time by getting organized.

"One morning I had a 9 a.m. aerobics class and after the work-out session I invited a few friends over for a piece of cake. (I know how stupid that sounds. You work like a fool for an hour and a half, then go home and eat cake.) I suppose I just wanted to show off.

"Everyone commented on how great the house looked. 'Did you get up at 4?' they asked. (I hadn't.) They were more impressed that I not only cleaned the house, but made a cake and started dinner, too.

"I'm not saying these things to brag, only to let you know that when things are planned and organized you can do everything faster and with less mental, physical, and emotional stress. The rest of that day was mine to enjoy. But even on the days when I go to work (I work part-time) I have more relaxed free time than I've ever had before."

Here's another testimonial: "Since you showed me how to plan menus and to shop using a master list, I have saved eight hours this month. (I kept track)." Planning and organization saves time. If you don't have time to plan menus it's probably because you're making too many last-minute dashes to the store (or the neighbor's) to pick up a few things for dinner. If you spent a few minutes planning and preparing a shopping list and went shopping once, for the next week or two you never have to set foot in a store! *That's* how she saved eight hours.

Here's another: "Dovetailing is everything you promised. I spend about 1/3 less time in my kitchen now. Dovetailing not only helps me cook faster, but clean-up is easier and faster, too."

A busy radio personality had this to say: "I tried your ideas for organizing my kitchen. I'm saving at least one hour a week by not having to look for things! It's great. I'm anxious to try your suggestions for shopping, entertaining, and meal planning so I can save even *more* time!"

The best way to use this book and to start realizing some of these benefits is to read it cover to cover. Then, follow the timetable in Chapter 4. This is only a guideline, however. You can work at your own speed, doing the job quicker or more slowly.

The book is also designed so each chapter, even when used independently, helps you save time. It only follows, then, the more chapter ideas you implement and coordinate, the more time you'll save. This format is helpful, too, if you want to use the book as a future reference.

An introductory warning: I make fun of a lot of gadgets in this book. Please, take it good naturedly. So what if I crack jokes about your ice-cream scoop (the one with the built-in defrosting element), your goose-feather pastry brush, or your sauerkraut forks? And whose business is it, anyway, if you save used plastic wrap and cardboard tubes? The purpose of this book is to help you get out of the kitchen. If you can accomplish that without tripping over your zucchini corer, your green peppercorn grinder, or your sonic key finder (the "clap and your keys start beeping" variety) well, you go right ahead and enjoy them.

Also, I put heavy emphasis on the word "you" in this book. Please interpret that to mean anyone who is warm, literate (and that's optional), and breathing. The best way to escape from your kitchen is to divide up the work so no one is sentenced to hard labor.

This book doesn't take long to read. Just think—all the knowledge you need to escape from your kitchen is just a few hours away. You can be the "commander in chef." Go for it and let freedom ring.

chapter 1

VILFREDO PARETO AND YOU

"Exactly why," you may ask, "is Vilfredo Pareto being discussed in a kitchen book?" Go ahead. Take a wild guess. If you think Vilfredo Pareto was a) one of Julia Child's Cordon Bleu instructors; b) the name of a fancy Italian potato peeler; or c) the concession vendor at La Scala . . . well, let me put it this way: if you were on a TV game show and had given one of those answers, you would probably have received some "lovely parting gifts" instead of cash, prizes, and a trip for two to Hong Kong.

Actually, Vilfredo Pareto was an Italian sociologist who studied tax logs in Florence. (Sounds stimulating, doesn't it?) Anyhow, what Vilfredo discovered has become a hot topic in business circles these days. As a matter of fact, several important books and this chapter, by the way, could not have been written without him.

You will, more than likely, recognize this discovery as the 80-20 principle. Everyone from economists and time consultants to salesmen and one-minute managers has applied this theory to his or her field of endeavor. And it has a lot to do with helping you escape from your kitchen. Here's how.

Vilfredo noticed that 20 percent of the tax payers paid 80 percent of the personal property taxes. So what? let me go on. If you translate that finding into your own fields of endeavor you'll learn that 20 percent of your efforts will bring 80 percent of the results, while the remaining 20 percent of the results would come from 80 percent of your efforts.

Here are some specific adaptations: 20 percent of the items in a grocery store bring in 80 percent of the profits; 20 percent of the food you regularly purchase is used to prepare 80 percent of your meals; 20 percent of the gadgets in your kitchen help you prepare 80 percent of your meals; 20 percent of the time you spend in your kitchen brings 80 percent of the desired results; 20 percent of the storage spaces in your kitchen are used 80 percent of the time.

Think about your vast cookbook and recipe collection. You probably use only 20 percent of those recipes 80 percent of the time. (Of course, the 80-20 principle is an approximation, but I think you'll find it is generally accurate.)

Vilfredo's discovery really had an impact on me when I realized I could operate my kitchen very effectively with only 20 percent of the food, gadgets, and recipes I keep in the kitchen. And to think I can cut down on the time I spend in my kitchen and still get 80 percent of the desired results—why that discovery is the greatest thing since the invention of gray tube socks! Certainly I'm not suggesting that you toss out your crock-pot, the Tabasco sauce, the gravy boat, and the banana split dishes. Rather, I'm suggesting that you separate the men from the boys, so to speak.

Through the course of the next few chapters, I'll show you how to decide which items fall into that high-priority 20 percent category and which are low-pay-off goods. When you discover what those preeminent 20 percent grocery items are—the ones you use 80 percent of the time—imagine the hours and frustration you'll save when you learn how to never run out of those things again!

Chances are ten to one you've complained about some feature in your kitchen: not enough drawers, no counter space, too few cupboards, etc. but when we finish prioritizing your kitchen equipment and kitchen space, you'll see how adequate your kitchen actually is. With the Pareto principle we'll open up functional areas of working space you never knew you had.

Whether you're operating out of a studio efficiency kitchen, or one that's "Cuisinized" to the max, there are four simple steps you must take to get your escape plan into action:

1. Discard and sort
2. Designate work centers
3. Prioritize your equipment and storage spaces
4. Put the equipment into the proper centers

Since I'm a confessed "Organized Housewife" I probably owe you an explanation as to why I'm going to begin with #3. I figure if you have a basic understanding of the prioritizing principles you'll have an easier time when you discard and sort, because you'll be more objective about the worth of a particular kitchen gadget. Rest assured, when it comes time to actually *do* the prioritizing, I'll be with you to show you exactly how it's done. Fair enough? Okay, here we go.

GIMME AN A

In his book *How to Get Control of Your Time and Your Life*, Alan Lakein gave the modern world the *ABC* method of prioritizing. Simply stated, this is a means whereby you prioritize the things you have to do: *A* being the most important, *C* being the least important.

While his hypothesis relates to time management, I think it also has an application to "things" management as well. In the parentheses under each category I give specific (however personal) examples.

A = HIGH VALUE

(Hamburger, measuring cups and spoons, dishwashing detergent, trash can, aspirin, cereal bowls, and the words, "I'll fix dinner tonight"—spoken by anyone else, including the parrot.)

B = MEDIUM VALUE

(Peanut butter and jelly, jar scraper, plastic wrap, muffin pans, colander, slotted spoon, and Betty Crocker's Good and Easy Cookbook.)

C = LOW VALUE

(Corn-on-the-cob holders, olive spears, old drip pans you're going to clean up when you find the time, bamboo steamer [except when used as a wall decoration] egg piercer separator, chestnut roaster, cheese cuber, and the set of six stainless steel lobster scoop forks.)

For the past few years I've been associated with the Charles R. Hobbs' Corporation, giving Dr. Hobbs' nationally famous Insight on Time Management seminars. Dr. Hobbs, who is also the author of *Time Power*, uses the *A-B-C* method of prioritizing, though he designates *A* as vital; *B* as important; and *C* as limited value (but some value). then he adds a *D* category, which I would like to include here.

D = TOTAL WASTE

("Girlie" ice cube molds, brown paper bags filled with brown paper bags, corn-on-the-cob butterers, and a "Do Not Immerse" electric anything.)

I like corn on the cob just as much as the next guy but that one piece of produce is responsible for more junk. Corn-on-the-cob dishes (each one holds one ear of corn), corn-on-the-cob holders, corn-on-the-cob butterers, corn-on-the-cob huskers, corn-on-the-cob kernel removers, (looks like a shoe horn and works better when used as one). When you think how often you actually eat corn on the cob you can see the futility of keeping all this plunder stored, moved, cleaned, inventoried, and replaced.

As you go through the discard and sort process that I'll describe in a minute, keep the *ABCD* prioritizing system in mind. Continually ask yourself: Is this gadget or foodstuff vital? Do I use it 80 percent of the time? Is it worth storing in a prime, high-priority area? Do I frequently move it to get to other more important things? What would happen if I got rid of this or removed it from the kitchen?

A's contribute daily (or at least several times a week) to what you want most—good, nourishing food served in a tidy kitchen. Keep your focus on that priority 20 percent where the highest payoff is.

If you've ever been hit on the head by a falling bag of powdered sugar; if you have three opened boxes of baking soda sitting around; if you're beginning to have symptoms of claustrophobia—or any other phobia—while working in your kitchen; I think it's safe to say you've got too many *C*'s and *D*'s sitting in, under, around, and throughout your kitchen. Those *C*'s and *D*'s bury the *A*'s and *B*'s, wasting large amounts of your time, energy, and money.

The more feckless junk you have in your kitchen the more time you have to spend doing even a simple task. Let's say you want to stir a pot of bubbling spaghetti sauce. In your quest for a wooden spoon you have to dig with the determination of an archaeologist to uncover your prey. Wouldn't it be easier to get rid of some of the junk, e.g. the bent beater from the electric mixer? (You know, the one that chewed up a spatula when it was turned on high.) And, why do you hang on to those spoons that were gnawed in the garbage disposer? In addition to the clutter, you rip up the corners of your mouth every time you try to eat with one. Then there are the bottles of vitamins, the three-volume set of *Eggplant Cookery*, and the once-shiny cookie sheets that now look like the dark side of the moon, both in color and texture. Every time you need something important and useful you have to move all this junk just to get to it.

To quote Don Aslett, author of *Clutter's Last Stand*, "Clutter makes everything take longer." Think about that the next time you run out of Crisco, or Pringles, or Cool Whip, or coffee, or margarine, or. . . . You'll never again have to make the decision, "Should I wash this container out and keep it, or just throw it away?" Save time—get rid of it!

You can open up functional areas of working and storage space for *A*'s by reducing the number of *C*'s and eliminating your *D*'s. Try removing all *C*'s and *D*'s from your kitchen and you know what will happen? Probably nothing. But you will experience that same feeling of relief you enjoyed the last time two of the kids went to the movies and the other two had sleepovers at someone else's house.

DISCARD AND SORT?
BAG IT!

The four-bag or box method is the best way to speed through any dejunking or sorting process. In a nutshell, here's how it works. Using four containers (boxes or large plastic trash bags) give each a specific function:

1. **Trash.** Things that no one would want or could use—e.g., expired coupons, dead batteries, warped pans, glass measuring cups with illegible or nonexistent red writing.

2. **Give away or sell.** Too good for the trash but you don't want. These are usually *C*'s and *D*'s—e.g., a bunny Jell-O mold; your collection of bud vases; that ceramic teapot without a lid you were someday going to make into a centerpiece, a planter, or a light fix-

ture; the thin warped cookie sheet you've used and burned cookies on for years.

3. **Put away.** These are things you need to keep but not in the kitchen. Or they're *C*'s that can easily be stored elsewhere—e.g., the Christmas elf butter mold, displaced toys, the 40-piece snack and chip dip set, empty Mason jars, and the "giraffe" recipe holder your son made for you in Cub Scouts out of a clothespin, a dowel, and a can filled with plaster of Paris. You really wouldn't have to put this away, except it's being replaced by the new recipe holder he made for you in school for Mother's Day—a fork standing up in a can filled with plaster of Paris.

4. **Don't know.** (The *pièce de résistance!*) Here lie the countless *C*'s and *D*'s; you can't live with them but you're not sure you can live without them, either—e.g., dull knives which you've promised yourself since your first wedding anniversary you'd have sharpened, but somehow you found it easier just to buy new knives; state-of-the-art electric candle with a Christmas-tree-light "flame" (complete with Dairy Queen curly-Q)—ordinarily you wouldn't keep this but it was given to you as the "Room Mother of the Year" award; the salad spinner (still in its box) that has yet to take a tumble; the single-serving casserole dish that's too small for you to use now, but it's part of a matching set and it "just might come in handy" when the kids leave home.

Why Bother With Boxes?

Now, why exactly does this system work? It does three things:

1. **The containers keep you from procrastinating regarding the job.** With each category by your side there'll be no reason to waste time running things back and forth to other places, such as taking the pliers back to the garage, bringing folded towels to the bathroom, and depositing your daughter's current events clippings into her book bag. You just stand in one spot and quickly discard and sort.

Another way we procrastinate is in making those heart-rending decisions. If you find yourself fondling that pig-shaped cookie jar that belonged to your mother and you just can't decide what to do with it, place it carefully into the I Don't Know Box. You're not going to get rid of the pig, you're just going to put it on "hold" for a while. For now, let's free up some space in your kitchen for purposes more important than storage.

2. The bags or boxes enable you to stop the project in progress without having the whole room torn up. This is especially important for a person whose eyes are bigger than her belly, so to speak. She starts out with vim, vigor, and vitality, but halfway through the project, somewhat comatose, she poops out—weary, weather-beaten, worn, wobegone, and wretched.

3. Since you never leave the kitchen, you won't be sidetracked by the TV, the afghan you're working on, the magazine that just arrived in the mail, or interruptions by other family members. Why interruptions? If you're like me, when buried in a project, especially a kitchen *cleaning* project, there's nary a soul for miles around. Seems like everyone steers clear of the project, for fear I'll try to round up a fledgling crew. But, if I leave the kitchen or even raise my head for a flash second, everyone thinks I'm fair game. "Will you make me a sandwich?" (Said as if auditioning for a "READ THIS AND CRY" ad.) "Mom, I don't have anything to wear," spoken in the woeful tones of an abandoned child. And my favorite, "Mom, Jeffrey's bugging me." What I wouldn't give for a black and white striped shirt and a loud whistle.

The four boxes keep you somewhat isolated and help you concentrate your efforts on the task at hand.

As you dejunk your kitchen remember to place heavy emphasis on determining those *A*'s and *B*'s. Kitchen space is much too valuable, especially in terms of time, to waste it storing a bunch of *C*'s and *D*'s.

At a Tupperware party a while back, one of the guests was protesting that she just couldn't buy any more Tupperware because she had no more room to store it. The wise Tupperware lady simply said, "Tupperware is made to be used, not stored."

The same goes for kitchen spaces—especially the handy spots. If your kitchen is tiny, you may only have room for the *A*'s and a few *B*'s. (That's okay—you'll still be able to get that 80 percent result.) With more room you can store *A*'s, *B*'s, and *C*'s. No matter the size of your kitchen, though, I always recommend eliminating ALL *D*'s. They waste your time, energy, and money. So, give them to a neighbor and let them clutter up *her* house! (Or take pity on her and donate this junk to a charity or thrift store.)

PICK YOUR M.O.

Now that you're a convert to the system, here are some methods (sort of variations on the theme) to help you unclutter your kitchen. Depending upon your personality, you can choose the "fast fix" method, the "party method," or several tempting alternatives in between.

Fast Fix

This procedure is best for those folks who find themselves knee-deep in the shallow spots. Sometimes the mess gets so bad, it's hard to continue functioning. Granted, this is only a temporary solution, it will cure the symptoms, but eventually you'll have to deal with the cause.

Here's how it works: You'll need some large plastic trash bags or cardboard cartons, two large, *clean* plastic wastebaskets, and a container for trash. Moving along one wall at a time, deposit *everything* into the trash bags or cartons. Place dishes, silverware, glasses, gadgets, etc. in one of the large plastic wastebaskets. Any recognizable and fresh-smelling food goes in the other plastic wastebasket.

Use the trash container sparingly at this point, however. Toss in only obvious pieces of garbage, i.e., crumpled pieces of paper, soiled napkins, hard, dried-up doughnuts, empty cans, etc. *Do not*—I repeat, DO NOT—look for garbage. Don't look through old magazines deciding whether or not to discard them; don't eye every scrap of paper to discover its value, or lack thereof. If you happen to stumble across something that shouts, "I AM TRASH," then toss it in the wastebasket. The object is to clear the area quickly.

Yes, this is going to make things hard to find, but they were probably buried anyway. Put the containers of dishes and food on the floor by the sink, or in a corner somewhere, throw out the trash, and put the remaining bags or cartons in an out-of-the-way spot.

When time permits put away the foodstuff and wash the dishes. Then using snatches of time if necessary, sit down with each of the bags and go through it, using the four-box method.

If clutter is interfering with your ability to function, then this system may be just what you need. It's quick and easy, and there's no turning back once it's done. It forces you into action.

Toss-It, Move-It

This is simply the four-container method taken one box at a time. It's sort of a nit-picking way to eliminate your clutter—slow, but great for people who don't have large blocks of time in which to work at home. Start with a trash basket, and just wander around the kitchen, poking through drawers, shelves, and cupboards, pulling out only those things you want to discard. When the discarding is completed, do the same thing again, pulling out things that don't belong. Several days later you're ready to repeat the process, ferreting out the stuff you want to sell or give away. Continue in this manner until the job is completed.

Tidbit

The tidbit method is ideal for those who can't stand to be in a mess for long or who have a tendency to give out before the job is finished. Using the basic four small containers, you simply go through the kitchen one shelf at a time, one drawer at a time, one corner at a time. This, too, can be slow, but it breaks the job down into bite-sized pieces.

Prove It

This is an interesting method, to say the least, and works extremely well in the kitchen. All you do is box up everything in a given closet, cupboard, or drawer. Put a date on the container. As you need things, you pilfer them from the box and put them away. Whatever remains in the box after six months is given away, sold, or discarded. (I know a family who does this on a regular basis. They swear by it!)

Pile It

This method is beloved of children, and isn't actually a way to get rid of the mess, but it helps you live with the mess while you're working on it. All you do is make piles. Articles of clothing, linens, etc., go in one pile or area, papers and books in another, food products in another, and dishes in another. Then attack each pile with the four-container method. This may be all the impetus you'll need to get started on your clutter reduction program.

Let's Party!

The party method is perfect for those who can't part with anything. Do it with a friend or friends. It's much easier to get rid of
things when you've got someone encouraging you, particularly if
she has a devil-may-care attitude. She can help you decide about
the value of certain items.

"An electric caramelizer?" your friend asks. "Well, who
knows," you reply, "someday I just might want to make creme brulée." With no better defense than "someday I might," your own
words (if not your friend's arguments) should convince you that
the electric caramelizer is at best a *C*, probably a *D*. Besides, if you
make creme brulée at home, what new and exotic dish will you order when you go out to eat?

Since many of us curry the approval of others, friends can
sometimes embarrass us into parting with stuff. When Mary un-
covers your novelty cake pan collection (you know, the ones
shaped like Yogi Bear, Winston Churchill, and a lunar landing mod-
ule) and wonders out loud if you're brain dead, of course you'll part
with them. Or, maybe you'll concede to storing them in a less functional area. (Thank heaven Mary didn't see the fifteen-piece piano
pan complete with piano bench and candelabrum!)

Whichever method you choose, do it with the zeal of the glad-
iator. Initially you may experience feelings and thoughts like: "As
soon as I get rid of that battery-operated self-stirring saucepan, I'll
break my arm or something. Then I'll wish I had it back." It's okay
to feel that way. I'm sure gladiators were scared, too. But that didn't
stop them.

Getting things prioritized and discarded has a cathartic effect. Pretty soon your cold feet will warm up as you discover how
fast you can find things and put them away. You won't dread cooking so much and you'll likely plan more thoughtful, and thus, more
nutritious, appealing meals. Trust me on this one. Get rid of your
Beechwood lemon reamer, your English muffin breaker, and your
baked potato puffer, and see if I'm not a woman of my word!

chapter 2

WHAT'S THE STORY ON STORAGE?

If Fred and Ginger were in search of the perfect dip, could they find it in your refrigerator? Oh, sure, they could probably find it, but could they find it without spilling leftover glasses of milk, without discovering anything gray and furry, and without doing bodily harm?

When you open a cupboard door do you experience the sensation of releasing a sluice gate and wish that just once the peanut butter chips, dried prunes, and Oreo cookies would stay perched on that shelf or crammed in that corner?

Reaching for the bottle of vanilla, do you schlepp through sedimentary layers of two-alarm chili sauce, coriander seeds, mango paste, and freeze-dried horseradish?

When you announce that you're fixing dinner, does your three-year-old ask, "What you fixing, Mommy? Hot dogs?"

I hate to throw ants on your picnic, but even though you've discarded and sorted, keeping mostly *A*'s and *B*'s (and a few *C*'s) in your kitchen, things are still a little haphazard, aren't they? (It's sort of like getting the lead in the school play and finding out you have to wear tights.) But hang in there, kid, the worst is over! Discard and sort was only the first step of your journey, albeit the toughest!

Referring to the timetable on page 2 you'll see that the next step (after discarding and sorting) is to designate work centers, i.e., mixing center, sink center, cooking center, serving center, refrigerator center.

With these work centers in operation, all equipment and supplies needed for a certain job (or series of jobs) are organized and stored exactly where the job is done. In the following chapters, we'll set up each center and learn the specific requirements of each. But for now, let's go into some general storage basics that apply for all five work centers. That way, when it comes time to reach out and touch something, you'll have a good idea where to start.

Think about all the things in your kitchen that are frequently misplaced or missing. Stuff like: a sharpened pencil near the phone, the kitchen scissors, the plastic lid for your Stor-Savr, and the chocolate chips you were going to use for Friday night's dessert.

Aside from the sheer frustration of not being able to locate something, you're wasting valuable time, energy, and money on search, rescue, or replacement missions. Then, there's the time- and energy-draining cross-examination, trial, and conviction of the guilty party. Avoid all that waste by keeping these four storage principles in mind:

1. Store things where they are first used.
2. Store items with motions in mind.
3. Store things in well-defined, well-confined places.
4. Label.

These four principles should be applied when arranging any work center, so let's tackle them one at a time.

POINT OF FIRST USE

Most of us, assuming that we're acting in an organized, efficient manner, put all the food in one cupboard, all the pots and pans in another, and we usually have a drawer or two stuffed with gadgets like the potato peeler, the nutmeg shaver, the clam opener, wooden spoons, and so on. Dishes and glassware are normally placed together in yet another cupboard.

What's wrong with that? Well, to get the roasting pan you get down on your knees, move three saucepans, the electric quiche pan, the hot dog fryer, and the mini-cooker that french fries one large shrimp at a time. To find the potato peeler your fingers have to do the walking (usually a marathon) to find it in the gadget drawer. You go to the pantry to get the potatoes and head back to the sink to pare them. To serve the roast you risk life, limb, and the pursuit of happiness to climb up in the dish storage area to unearth the platter.

I have read many university studies that have shown how much time can be saved by a simple reorganization of equipment and supplies. One study revealed a whopping 45 percent reduction in the time spent. This was all made possible by storing things where they were first used. So instead of classifying things by what they are, consider where they're used first. Now this doesn't mean that you store your Ivory Liquid in the sink, but it does mean—especially if you have kids—that you store the garlic press with the Play Doh.

Of course, there are things like measuring cups and measuring spoons, certain types of pans, stirring spoons, can openers, etc. that are used first in more than one place. Sometimes you use an item by the sink, let's say, and sometimes in the mixing center. If you can't afford the space (or the money) to provide duplicates, then simply put the item where it is *most often* used first.

THE MOTION IS CARRIED

Not only should you store things at the point of first use, you should also store them with motions in mind. Here's what I mean.

While I'm discarding and sorting, I get a good feel for which items are *A*'s, which are *B*'s and so on. (I eliminate *all D*'s.) Those *A*'s and *B*'s are treated with tender loving care and are given one-motion storage. That means I can reach in and grab the paring knife, let's say, with one motion and put it back with one motion. One-motion storage is mandatory for all *A*'s; great for *B*'s—but not necessary unless you have room; okay, but not needed for *C*'s.

To make one-motion storage a bit more logical, I prioritize kitchen space the same way I prioritize kitchen equipment. Check the following illustration. This is roughly how I'd prioritize it.

A spaces are always found in prime areas (between hip and eye level) and are located so you can reach in and grab things quickly and return them quickly, i.e., front half of top drawers, front of eye level to hip level shelves, top shelf in the refrigerator. This is, however, your decision. Since I'm 5 feet 7 inches tall, I ranked the front of shelves #2 and #5 (see illustration) as *A*'s. If you're 5 feet 2 inches, they would likely be *B*'s or even *C*'s, maybe. So the *ABC* method of prioritizing is both a matter of opinion and your particular circumstances.

It helps me to think of my kitchen in terms of usage and storage areas. *A* and *B* priority spaces are usage spaces. Don't clutter them up with *C* items. To get true one-motion storage, put *A* things in *A* places and *B* things in *B* places, and so on. WARNING: Keep in mind that we're talking about an ideal arrangement and as we all know that is rarely possible. Just take care of your *A*'s first. If there's no room for anything else, so what? You'll have 80 percent of your activities covered. Also, we'll deal with specific problems a little later.

You make the most from your available time and space by storing those *A*'s in convenient spots, keeping them clean and in good repair. Sometimes it helps to have a few duplicates of impor-

Prioritize your kitchen space the same way you do your kitchen equipment.

tant *A* tools, food, and cleaning supplies. It isn't worthwhile to give a *C* (the doughnut fryer) a handy, convenient place of honor in your kitchen, unless, of course, you're the Dunkin' Donuts man. On the other hand, an *A* deserves a reach-in-and-grab-it-quickly location.

For example, my steam canner, pectin, and Ball canning book are *C*'s most of the year. but during summer and early fall months, they move up to *A*'s. Now, does that mean I give them *A* storage spots? Absolutely not. *A* places are reserved only for those 20 percent of things that are in constant need. Their use is basically un-fluctuating.

In summary, here's a rundown:

A's = one motion

B's = one motion (when possible), two motions, bend or stretch slightly

C's = two or more motions; bend, stretch, or walk; rummaging is okay for this category.

D's = Shame on you! A note will be sent home to the children of all readers who are still hanging on to D's!

DIVVY IT UP

My personal motto is (and if I had the capabilities I would print this in type size normally reserved for presidential resignations):

"Give everything a well-defined, well-confined place and always return it to that exact place."

That, ladies and gentlemen, is what this book is all about. It's the real secret to escaping from your kitchen.

What are well-defined, well-confined places? Just ask my mom for the potato masher and she'll respond with, "Top drawer next to the sink, third compartment on the right hand side. It's next to the potato peeler and the paring knife." Disgusting? No, no, no. It's a wonderful orchestration of kitchen efficiency. How come?

There are several reasons why giving things specific places is important. First, when the potato masher is always in the top drawer next to the sink, third compartment on the right hand side, every time you reach for it, your hand responds as if it were attached to R2-D2. Your motions become smooth, though deliberate, and automatic. You can always find the potato masher (or whatever). It is never intertwined and tangled with the baked potato nails, the handle of the spatula, or the gravy ladle. It is always at the ready—hassle-free.

Second, when things are given a well-contained area to inhabit, they stay there. There's no jostling to other parts of the drawer when it's slammed shut. When things are compartmentalized they become prisoners and in solitary confinement, and stay put.

Third—and highly important—if other people in the family learn the specific places where things belong and always find them there, they begin to have a picture in their minds: the proper place to put something. Of course, and here's the catch, this takes some consistency on your part.

When I first set things up, every time I opened a cupboard or drawer and found something out of place, I very quickly and quietly put it back where it belonged. I decided since I was the one who wanted order and the free time to show for it, I would be the one responsible for maintaining the system, at least in the beginning. Besides, it only takes a second or two.

In the long run this practice has really paid off. The kids can put things back with the same precision I can, and they put them back where they belong. This isn't as pretentious as it sounds. Though they *know* where everything goes I still have to tell the kids to put things away. And yes, sometimes I use my best town crier voice. A dash of despotism is also effective.

Finally, you know what a mess people make when they're looking for things? Well-defined, well-confined places prevent that. Again, your hand gravitates to just the spot where the desired item is being stored. No muss, no fuss.

The only tools you need for this beatific state are drawer dividers and lots of them. Drawer dividers come in all different sizes and colors, and you can mix and match them so they'll fill up any size drawer. Standard drawer dividers are readily available in department, discount, and variety stores, as well as large supermarkets everywhere. But aside from those typical drawer dividers, you can use anything that's square or rectangular in shape, and hollow: ice cube bins, four-sided napkin holders, liners for planters, cardboard boxes, baskets, dishpans (regular and restaurant sized), and kitty litter pans. Don't snicker. They are wonderful organizers and the big news is they now come in decorator colors. Drawer dividers

Use plenty of drawer dividers to give everything a well-defined, well-confined place.

sit on shelves to contain small bottles and packages, under sinks or on deep shelves to serve as slide-out "drawers" or trays. Drawer dividers are perfect for the refrigerator and even the junk drawer—which, by the way, is not long for this world.

LABEL, LABEL IF YOU'RE ABLE

Labeling has a lot of different applications. It can take the form of coding, that is, all yellow pencils belong in the kitchen, all colored ones go in the family room; all food marked with a red signal dot is being used as an ingredient for something this week—hands off. Or, more directly, labeling can mean actually listing the contents of drawers or shelves, and posting the list in or on each respective drawer or shelf so everyone knows exactly what goes where. To encourage family cooperation, many people label individual drawer dividers so Jr. knows the measuring cups go here, the pancake turner there, etc. I have also labeled (with permanent felt marker or nail polish) the kitchen scissors, stapler, phone book, etc. because we have duplicates in various rooms. When things are well-labeled there's never any confusion.

STORAGE FOR YOUR TENDER VICTUALS

We all store food. Some of you may have a small cache—say, an extra box or two of pistachio Jell-O, water chestnuts left over from when you didn't go through with your plans to make Mongolian Beef, Szechuan style, maybe a few boxes of macaroni and cheese, and some cans of liver-flavored dog food. Still others may have enough food to operate the San Diego Zoo and feed my husband for an entire year! (Now I'm not insinuating that Jim is an animal; let's just say after seventeen years of marriage I'm still wondering what leftovers are.)

In any event, if you're storing food on purpose or by accident you need to do it correctly. Here are some generic guidelines that will help you when it comes time to actually set up your work centers.

The purpose of storing food correctly is to ensure the quality of the food. In other words, you want your food to be acceptable in color, flavor, odor, and texture; when food is stored safely, waste is reduced and nutrition is optimum. There are several things that may affect food quality: excesses in temperature, moisture, light, time, dust, and pests such as insects and rodents. Because of the temperature, moisture, and light variables, we are frequently cautioned to store food in cool, dry, dark places. It's also wise to store food off the floor (two-three feet in flood-prone areas) in food-grade containers.

Many containers nowadays—including large plastic trash bags—are treated with chemicals and should not be used for food storage since the toxin may be transferred into the food. Containers that are suitable for food storage sometimes advertise that fact on the label. If you're in doubt, call or write to the container manufacturer and ask if it is approved for food use. Also, proper packaging allows for adequate ventilation and prevents condensation of moisture on packaging material.

To prevent unwanted pests, store food in clean glass, metal, or heavy plastic containers with tight-fitting lids. The receptacles should have no open seams or crevices.

If you have food that has been on your shelf for an extended period of time and you're unsure of the age of the product (and thus its desirability), check to see if there's an expiration date printed on the product.

There are two basic types of codes on food packaging—open and closed. An open code is a date you can read and understand. A closed code may look something like this: CJF 3113. This code can identify a number of things, i.e., date the product was manufactured, batch number, time of the day produced, expiration date, manufacturer's name, pull date, plant, vat number, packer, etc.

Each company has a different code and you need a key to be able to read it. While most companies probably won't send you their code key, they will tell you about the quality of a coded product.

Let's say you're wondering if those cans of creamed corn are still worth eating, or if the labels themselves would actually taste better and be more nutritious. If you write to the manufacturer (the address is on the package), give the code (usually found on the bottom). They'll write back and give you the information you requested.

If you want to learn the codes used in your supermarket, ask the employees or the store manager. Most of them have access to a master code to help them interpret the letters and numbers found on the products they sell.

There are also shelf life charts that you can refer to. Check your cookbooks, local school's home economics department, and the USDA. This, of course, is only practical if you can remember approximately when the food was purchased. Never taste anything you suspect may be tainted. Sometimes toxic food tastes and smells perfectly fine. Also, any suspected food you discard should be wrapped securely so animals won't be contaminated by it.

Storage Basics

Keep the following points in mind:

- Avoid storing food in opened containers.
- Clean up all spills immediately. Wipe off containers before storing on the shelf or in the refrigerator. (Do this after every use.)
- Household chemicals should not be stored near food. Some chemicals may affect flavor and odor of food.
- Don't store foods in cupboards where pipes are located. Condensation or leakage from the pipes can damage food. Also small openings around pipes are very attractive to insects and rodents.
- Seal all openings (such as around pipes) with caulking or stuff steel wool in the openings and cover securely with duct tape.
- When placing food on shelves or in the refrigerator, store newest food in back so the oldest item is used first.

- Canned foods should not be stored near the stove, radiator, or anything damp. Once opened, canned food should be transferred into a covered glass or plastic container and placed in the refrigerator.

- Food should not be stored near heat sources such as freezers, furnaces, and hot water heaters.

The USDA also makes these recommendations (especially for long-term storage items):

1. Take an inventory and keep it current. (I'll show you how, later.)

2. Make sure food is being rotated. (Use oldest food first.)

3. Throw away any leaking or bulged cans and unsealed packages.

4. Check bulk grains periodically for rodent or insect infestation.

5. Monitor the temperature in the refrigerator (34°-40° F), the freezer (below 0° F), and the storage area (average temperature should be above 32° F and below 70° F).

According to *Food Storage*, a booklet put together by the Utah State University extension service: "The lower the temperature, the longer the shelf life. Persons storing foods in a garage at an average temperature of 90° F should expect a shelf life less than half of what could be obtained in a cool basement at 60°-70° F."

Should you want further information about storing food safely, a good source is the USDA. Write to the Superintendent of Documents, Washington, DC 20402 and ask for a listing of USDA titles. The USDA also publishes an annual Yearbook of Agriculture which can be secured at your local library or from the USDA.

Another source is your local cooperative extension service. If you have a university nearby, call and ask if they have an extension office in your vicinity. They work in tandem with the USDA and can supply you with information pertinent to your particular clime, growing season, and native pests. etc.

It makes no difference what type of native pests you're dealing with—roaches, weevils, mice, or inmates who drop things at the point of *last* use. Apply these storage principles and cut loose those apron strings. Your escape is imminent.

chapter 3

PUTTING AN END TO THE KITCHEN MARATHON

Did you know you can train for a marathon right in your kitchen? That's right! A marathon, or a twenty-six-mile race. The average family cook walks about four and a half marathons a year just fixing dinner! If you'd like to save your training for the great out-of-doors (and have more time to do it) I'm about to knock off about forty miles from your current kitchen marathon training. This is made possible by organizing work centers that provide you with storage at the point of first use—and you *don't* need a kitchen large enough to harbor a small aircraft. Setting up only three areas will be more than adequate: sink center, cooking center, and mixing center. You can also add a serving and refrigerator center, or these can be easily incorporated into the other three.

When reading through the following lists of items for each center, remember that they are merely guidelines. The purpose of these lists is to give you a starting point when it comes time to actually set up each center. So, think for yourself. For example, the serving center list includes the toaster. Personally, we keep ours in the mixing center because I fix toast while I'm frying bacon and eggs. Also, I am not suggesting via these lists, that you need all these pieces of equipment. I personally own maybe 1/3 of this stuff and we're all alive, well, warm, and breathing.

21

To add extra storage space in the sink center, convert the decorative front panel into a tilt-out storage bin.

An over-the-sink dish drainer frees up counter space.

THE SINK CENTER

The sink center is where you wash food, dispose of garbage, clean up dishes, and get water for cooking. Here's a list of items often used first at the sink:

apple corer

aprons

bandages

can opener

canned soups (may also be stored in cooking center)

cleaning supplies (take necessary precautions)

coffee

coffeemaker

colander

cutlery

cutting board

dish cloths and towels

dish detergent

dish drainer, dishpan

dishes (unless stored in serving center)

double boiler (bottom only)

dried peas, beans, etc.

drinking glasses

fruit juicer

funnel

garbage container and liners

hand lotion

hand soap

immersion coil

kitchen scissors

liquid measuring cup, 1 quart

measuring cups and spoons

medicines (take necessary precautions)

melon ball cutter

onions

pan scourer

pans (those you usually add water to first)

paper bags (if used to line wastebasket)

paper towels

paring knives

pet food (that requires the addition of water)

pitchers

plant food and watering container

plate scraper

potatoes

rice

rubber gloves

silverware (unless stored in the serving center)

tea kettle

vegetable brush

vegetable peeler

vitamins

THE COOKING CENTER

You don't need to be a card-carrying genius to figure out that the cooking center is where you cook, but it's also where you store pots and pans, stir food, and test foods for thorough cooking. Here's a list of items normally used first at the cooking center:

A slide-out pan rack provides one-motion storage.

aluminum foil

baster

broiler pan

cake testing tool

canned foods (poured directly into pan on the stove)

canned vegetables

can opener

chafing dish

condiments (non-refrigerated)

cooked cereals

cooking forks and spoons

cooling racks

cutting board

deep fat fryer

double boiler (top only)

egg poacher (or store in sink center)

fire extinguisher

flour (for thickening gravy or coating meat or fish)

frying pans and covers

garlic press

griddle

instant rice

ladle

long-handled fork and spoon

measuring cups and spoons

microwave oven

oil

pancake turner

pasta

perforated spoon

plastic wrap

potato masher (or store in mixing center)

pot holders

pressure cooker

rice

roasting pan and cover

salt, pepper

saucepans and lids

seasoning mixes (poured

directly into pan on the stove)

serving dishes

serving trays, platters

slotted spoons

spices (poured directly into pan on stove)

tea (or store in sink center)

thermometers (meat, deep fat, candy)

timer

tongs

trivets (or hot pads to set hot dishes on)

wax paper

wire whip

wooden spoons

THE MIXING CENTER

The mixing center is simply a preparation area where you get things ready to eat. You mix, blend, beat, chop, stir, and combine ingredients in the mixing center, and since so much goes on here, you need a wide variety of tools, equipment, and food. Here's a list of mixing center ingredients:

aluminum foil

baking powder

baking sheets and pans

baking soda

biscuit mix

blender

bottle opener

bread pans

brown sugar

cake decorating equipment

cake mixes

cake pans

canisters

canned goods (not placed directly into a pan on the stove)

can opener

casserole dishes

Escape from the Kitchen

A simple wooden rack built on the end of a bank of cupboards is handy for spices or other small items.

chocolate

cocoa

cookbooks

cooking spoons and forks

cooling racks (or store in cooking center)

cornstarch

custard cups

cutters for biscuits and cookies

cutting board

dough scraper and cutter

egg beater

flavorings

flour and sifter

food grinder

food processor

freezer supplies (cartons, foil, freezer tape, marker)

garbage container and liners (optional, though it's nice to have one close by while you're preparing food)

graters

herbs

jams, jellies

jar scraper

Jell-O molds

knives and sharpener

lunch boxes and Thermos bottles

mallet
measuring cups and spoons
mixer
mixing bowls
molds (custard cups, rame-
kins, pudding steamers)
muffin pans
non-pareils
nuts
pancake mix
paper towels
pastry blender
pastry brush
pastry cloth
pastry tube
peanut butter
pie pans
plastic bags
plastic wrap
poultry shears
powdered milk
powdered sugar
prepared mixes
pudding pans
raisins

ricer
rolling pin
rubber scrapers
salad oil
salt and pepper
sandwich bags
scale
scissors
scoops
seasoning mixes (not placed
directly into a pan on the
stove)
shortening
sieves
skewers
spatula (for frosting cakes)
spices
spreads (nonrefrigerated)
syrup (or store in serving
center)
tapioca
vinegar
waxed paper
white sugar
wire whip

THE SERVING CENTER

The serving center is usually close to the stove, and is often combined with the cooking center. It should be handy to the eating area
because its purpose is to enable you to serve meals quickly and easily. This center is optional and is probably only worthwhile in a
large kitchen.

Here's a list of things to consider storing in your serving center, should you choose to have one. If not, incorporate these items into one of the other centers.

baked goods

beverages (bottled or canned)

bread

chips

coffee creamer

cookies

crackers

dishes*

dish pan (for transporting
   dishes to sink center)

fondue pot

glasses*

grill

jelly and jam

ladle

margarine

prepared cereals

salt and pepper

silverware*

sugar

syrup

tablecloths, placemats,
   napkins

table condiments

toaster

trivets

waffle iron

*Personally, I think it's best to store these starred items at the point of last use (the sink center) for ease in putting them away. Otherwise, if you're like me, you'll leave the dishes stacked on the counter "for now" until you have the time or the tendency to cart them back to the serving center.

A good mix is to keep the fine china, crystal, silver, etc. in the serving center and the everyday ware at the sink center.

THE REFRIGERATOR CENTER

The refrigerator center is, of course, where foods are kept cold or frozen and leftovers are stored. But it's also where sandwiches are sometimes made, and where cold desserts are served. Here's a list:

bread

can opener

cheese slicer

covered containers for leftovers

cutting board

dessert toppings

freezer wrap

ice bucket

ice-cream dishes

ice-cream scoop

jar scraper

knives

labels for frozen goods

marking pen

mixing spoons

plastic freezer bags

sandwich bags

In Chapter 4 you'll find step-by-step instructions for setting up your centers and will need to refer to these lists again. So mark these pages with a paper clip and you'll be able to flip to them quickly and frequently. In any case don't be overwhelmed. I'll also show you how to store all the trappings in a logical, efficient manner.

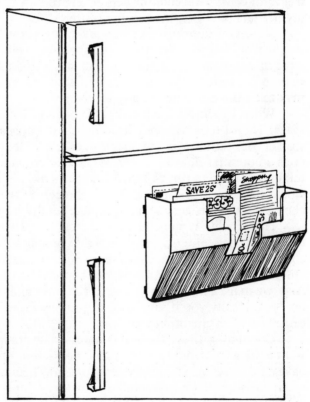

A magnetic refrigerator caddy holds everything from coupons to phone books.

ON LOCATION

The locations for the refrigerator center, sink center, and the cooking center are about as obvious as the Pope's religion. The sink center will be housed around the sink, the cooking center near the stove, and the refrigerator center will, of course, be next to the TV. (Just seeing if you were paying attention.) Actually, though, that wouldn't be a bad idea!

The rest of this chapter will help you streamline your existing kitchen without knocking out walls, pouring cement, and saying words the children shouldn't hear. But if you're getting ready to remodel or planning to build a house, Chapter 12, "By Design," will offer additional information.

Meanwhile, back in the kitchen, we've already located the refrigerator center, the cooking center, and the sink center. Now for my personal favorite, the mixing center.

Were you to prioritize the work centers, the mixing center would be at least an *A*. So, it's most important to take extra pains to store things properly here even if it means a slight inconvenience to the other centers. With a carefully placed mixing center you can maximize the efficiency of any kitchen.

When I go into a kitchen, the first thing I look for is counter space. Then I check for overhead and base cupboard areas. Any span of countertop with cupboards over and under I would consider as a potential mixing center. Whenever possible, I set up the mixing center between the stove and the sink. My second choice would be next to the stove. Third choice: by the sink. Fourth choice: by the refrigerator. Last choice: totally isolated.

Here's why. When checking the center's lists you'll notice that the mixing center, the sink, and the cooking center have many common entities. It only makes sense then to combine the three in order to cut down on the number of duplicates you need to store. Also, we make a lot of trips between the stove and the mixing center. So, logically you'll save a lot of time by locating the mixing center between the other two.

Combining these three has another advantage. When you want to fix a big "from scratch" meal, a casserole, or a dessert, you have a full-sized mixing center to work in. Then on those nights when you want to chop vegetables, etc. for a Chinese stir-fry, let's say, you have that same available space as a full-sized cooking center. You get twice the value from your counter space because you're doubling up on storage. It's by far the best arrangement.

Failing that, my second choice would be to set up a mixing center by the stove. The mixing center and the cooking center have the most often duplicated supplies and equipment and we cover more ground between these two centers than we do any others. Also, most of the cooked food we prepare requires some advance preparation—again calling together the services of the mixing center and the cooking center.

The sink center and the mixing center also have a few common tools but not quite as many as the cooking and mixing centers. Also, the sink is not used in food preparation as much as the stove is. For these reasons, this would be my third choice.

Years ago many homes were designed to combine the refrigerator and the mixing center. But, there are few reasons to work by the refrigerator. Most refrigerated items needed for food preparation can be gathered in one trip and there are not a lot of tools and equipment needed in the refrigerator center, which forces you to have dupes in other locations as well.

Finally, if your mixing center is isolated you will be forced to walk back and forth between centers, adding minutes and miles to your kitchen marathon.

To re-cap, here's a priority run-down on mixing center locations:

A = Between stove and sink
B = Next to cooking center
$C+$ = Next to sink
C = Next to refrigerator
$C-$ = Totally isolated

Locating the serving center is more or less a matter of opinion. Ideally (a rare occurrence) it should be close to the stove, the table, and the sink or dishwasher. That way you can set the table, cook, serve, and clean up in a logical sequence of motions.

Now, here's where opinion comes in. Our current kitchen (a real dog) makes that arrangement impossible, so I've chosen to keep the dishes, glasses, and silverware by the dishwasher (to facilitate putting them away) and the serving center food items are stored close to the table. You'll notice the food on that list requires no advance preparation. It is served exactly the way it is right to the dishes. Also, if you're in the habit of serving food directly from the stove onto individual plates, the dishes could be stored in the cooking center.

The "U"-shaped kitchen always wins the time and motion studies. Because of its tight design, the centers are all concurrent and easily accessible to each other. Even so, there is no such thing as a perfect arrangement. I've worked with people who have spent thousands of dollars on their kitchens but still I hear, "I wish I had done this or that." So, don't get discouraged. While no kitchen is 100 percent, it can be pretty close most of the time.

I like the attitude of a woman at one of my seminars. She said; "I'm putting a lot of your ideas to use. I'm still not perfect, but things are so much better."

My kitchen is surely not perfect, but now that it's organized correctly, it's "so much better." For example, I'm pretty much an old-fashioned cook. I cook from scratch most of the time and fix quick, family-style meals. Once in a while, I'll cook up a gourmet feast or some "continental cuisine," but most of the time it's strictly down-home style. So my kitchen is organized to satisfy that style of cooking. When I deviate from that standard, my kitchen is not quite as functional. But that's okay because 80 percent of the time it's close to perfect.

PAST IMPERFECT

Now, what if your mixing center is isolated and the stove has no counter space next to it? What if there are no overhead cupboards in your mixing center or by the sink? What if there's no place to set a mixing bowl after you've used it? How can you make awkward centers more functional?

If you're in dire circumstances, the first thing to do is to generously eliminate everything but those A's from your kitchen. That single effort will bring greater results than anything else.

Here are some other solutions. Let's say your mixing center is isolated from the cooking center and you can't combine the two areas. As long as you have a good mixing center, this arrangement isn't really as bad as it sounds. Here's what you do. Suppose you're making spaghetti sauce. Begin browning the meat, onions, and vegetables at the cooking center. Meanwhile, at the mixing center, combine the other sauce ingredients in a mixing bowl. After the meat is brown, drain off the fat and pour the prepared sauce over the meat and simmer. In other words, prepare everything at the mixing center and carry it to the cooking center when it's ready to be cooked or baked.

A wheeled cart can be useful in all the centers, if you have space for it. Next to a stove it can hold the electric frying pay, broiler pan, aluminum foil, bouquet of utensils, saucepans and lids, fire extinguisher, or any other items needed there.

A portable mixing center can be rolled wherever it's needed.

It can also serve as a portable mixing center. Gather needed supplies for a particular meal and place them on the shelves of the cart; the top can serve as extra counter space. A wheeled cart can also be used as a permanent mixing center, though you'll probably have room to store *A*'s only.

A portable bar is another storage solution. It can serve as a kitchen island, holding cookbooks, placemats, supplies, etc. It can also be used as a buffet or to supply extra counter space. In smaller kitchens, keep the bar in another room and roll it into the kitchen when you need extra work space. Or, shop for a free-standing cupboard to butt up against a wall, or use it as an island.

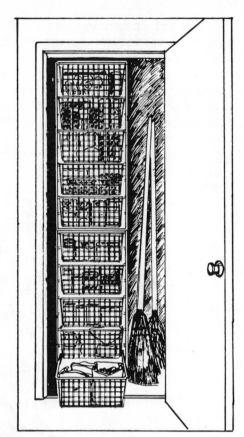

Stacking bin drawers provide
extra storage.

My sister, Judy, bought an unfinished chest of drawers for her kitchen. She painted it to match the kitchen decor so it's pretty as well as handy. The deep drawers hold bins of flour and sugar, table cloths, placemats, baking sheets, pans, food grinder, graters, lunch boxes, etc. and the chest is low enough to lend extra counter space to the kitchen.

Additional counter space can also be gained by having a board fitted to span the front half of the sink. Be sure the board only goes one-half to three-quarters of the way back, so you can still use the faucet. Also, have a backstop installed under the board (a piece of wood will do) so the board won't slide around or pop out while you're working on it. A board can be hinged to a wall and lowered only when needed, or have a pull-out board installed under a convenient counter-top. Or, open up a drawer and put a cutting board over it to give you a few more feet of working surface.

A fold-down table is a great space stretcher in small kitchens.

No place to set a mixing bowl once you've used it? There's no need to use precious counter space as a holding place for dirty dishes. A restaurant-sized dishpan or tall plastic wastebasket sits right on the floor by your working area or under the sink and holds dirty dishes until you're ready to wash them. (Rinse them off quickly, then place them in the holding container.) Or if you have room, a dishpan filled with soapy water sitting on the counter in your mixing center helps you clean up as you go.

If a sink isn't close to your mixing center you can pare vegetable and fruits on newspaper or freezer wrap in the mixing center and toss the scraps away. And if you have lots of storage space but poorly placed appliances, you can opt for mini versions placed wherever you want them (i.e., toaster/oven/broiler, hot plate, electric frying pan, mini refrigerator, mini microwave, immersion coil).

Good Housekeeping magazine offers another solution: If the area above your kitchen cupboards is enclosed by a soffit, you can replace the front piece with a sliding door, fabric, or a small hinged door (see illustration). If no soffit is installed, you can hang a curtain from the ceiling to conceal the storage area or install drop-down doors from a piece of molding installed on the ceiling. Just be sure the cupboard can withstand the extra weight. If not, the unit should be reinforced. Of course, soffit-area storage is best reserved for *C*'s.

Escape from the Kitchen

Convert a soffit into C-type storage areas by installing small hinged doors on the front panel.

One friend has a filing cabinet in her kitchen. The cabinet is decorated with paint and wallpaper and provides her with a pretty storage area for appliances, cereal boxes, serving trays, large bowls, and all sorts of cargo.

Standard open wooden shelves stacked up next to an unused wall provide pantry storage for food, bins, cookbooks, pans, appliances—whatever. Sometimes just changing the position of the refrigerator or the table will open up enough room to house a new counter top or a few extra shelves.

So far I've been talking in generalities, but in the next few chapters we'll get into specifics: how to store everything from the spices to the SOS pads. Once your centers are physically fit there'll be plenty of time for your own fitness program. You'll even have time for Phyllis Diller's favorite exercise: a good, brisk sit!

chapter 4

SETTING UP IS AS EASY AS C-C-C

We live in an age of megabucks, megatrends, and mega-abbreviations. We've got the NCAA (not to be confused with the NAACP); the ASPCA (not to be confused with the AARP); and there's the NFL (which, according to my husband is not to be confused with the USFL). Wait. There's more: CEO's (who, when they're not involved with R and D are getting some R and R); CPA's (most of whom belong to the NAA); UFO's (reported to the USAF); and, lest we forget, those dreaded POSSLQ's (persons of the opposite sex sharing living quarters) brought to us by the US Census Bureau. And where do POSSLQ's go when they feel they've been discriminated against? To the ACLU, naturally.

Yes, over the years we've saved countless hours, millions of dollars, and miles of typewriter ribbon just by using abbreviations. For instance, when referring to the MTUOP as such, instead of as the mobile training unit out for parts, you can save writing twenty-four letters or 3.783 seconds every time it comes up in a conversation. Staggering.

The purpose of abbreviations is not always brevity—with the exception, perhaps, of the ALROS or American Laryngological, Rhinological, and Otological Society. The letters, I suppose are just plain easier to remember; except perhaps, with the ASTSECNAVAIR or the Assistant Secretary of the Navy for Air.

If you've been confused as I have with all this jargon maybe a little simplicity would help. I'm going to show you an abbreviated system that's so incredibly easy, all you have to do is remember three **C**'s. These are the **C-C-C**'s of setting up a work center.

> **C** = Clean
> **C** = Cull
> **C** = Categorize

C-ING THE MIXING CENTER

Assuming you've done all the preliminary discarding and sorting as outlined in Chapter 1, you're almost ready for your first **C.**

But, before you slide head first into the base, so to speak, I want you to go in with your eyes open. We're starting with the mixing center because it's the most important center, it contains a large portion of your kitchen equipment, and it's the hardest, messiest part of your escape. However, setting up a good mixing center is what makes that escape largely possible.

To make it less overwhelming I have broken down the job into manageable portions so you don't have to up-end the kitchen for three and one-half weeks.

I'll describe the fastest method first; then, after you've read through the entire process, I'll give you a piecemeal approach. That way, if you're working away from home, if you have preschoolers, or if you're just plain faint-hearted—or even lazy—you can still reach the summit without raising dust and working up a sweat.

Even so, it would be a good idea to plan simple, quick meals for the week you're working on the mixing center. Soup, sandwiches, salads, fast foods, stuffed baked potatoes, crock-pot meals, or casseroles would be good choices. Once you've made out your menus, segregate the ingredients for these forthcoming meals so they won't get lost in the shuffle.

Just promise the family paté of pheasant supreme, asparagus brulée, and Caribbean pineapple flambé after the project is completed. Whatever you entice them with, be sure the name of at least one dish has that little mark (´) over a vowel somewhere. That simple accent is what turns smooshed-up goose liver into paté de foie gras. It works every time.

C = Clean

As soon as you've decided what area in your kitchen to earmark for the mixing center, clean it out. Take everything out of the designated cupboards. If possible, relocate this equipage to other cupboards or simply corral it in boxes so it's out of the way. If you suspect some of these items will be used in the mixing center, place them on an adjacent counter or nearby table.

When the area is cleared, it's time for a thorough cleaning. Wash and dry cupboard interiors, shelves, and door fronts. Ditto with the drawers. Wash and dry the counter-tops, backsplash, and the mixing center wall. If desired, cover the drawers and shelves with shelf liner. Once the mixing center is clear and clean you're ready for step 2.

However, if you want to call it a day, this would be a good stopping point. Yes, you'll have to rummage a little to find the things you pulled from the mixing center, but at least the whole kitchen isn't torn up.

If, in the process of cleaning, you've set aside things that will be used at the mixing center, go ahead and put them away in the clean shelves and drawers. Don't worry about organizing at this point. We're just getting things out of sight.

C = Cull

Flip back to pages 25-27 and take a few minutes to scan the mixing center list of suggested foods and equipment. Put a red check mark or draw a circle around any of the items you currently use. Do you use it first at the mixing center? If so, tick it off. Is there any mixing center gear you normally use that's not included on the list? If so, pencil it in the margin.

Remember, the mixing center is an *A*. So if you've only got one can opener, let's say, and you use it in two different locations, the mixing center wins out. It's okay to slightly inconvenience the other centers. (You can always keep the electric can opener in the mixing center and a small hand-held model at the sink center.) The mixing center always has priority over the other centers.

Now, with your personalized list in front of you, cull all the items you've designated as belonging to the mixing center. Put them on the mixing center counter and put the overflow on a nearby table. You may even want to set up a card table to keep things handy.

Keep your eyes peeled for any *C* and *D* priority gadgets and foodstuffs you may have passed over in your discard and sort session, and cut your losses. These impulse purchases were a waste of money; admit it and go on. Don't let impulse dupe you again by robbing you of needed space. (This speculation is based on the assumption that no red-blooded American shopper in her right mind would actually *plan* to buy an electric duck plucker with revolving rubber fingers that plucks fifty-three ducks an hour.) It's time to let go and live.

Once you've rounded up all the component parts—and don't forget the ones you may have stashed away in the mixing center after your cleaning session—it's time to begin step #3.

C = Categorize

Step three is the most time-consuming so let's break it down into at least two work days. To finish up your culling project, you need to categorize all the mixing center chattel into three priority piles. If you're going to wrap up your day's work after this prioritizing, it's best to use three boxes or containers, so you won't have a quagmire in the interim. And even if you *do* keep plugging away, I strongly suggest you put all the smaller (and nonfood) *C* priority things in a box.

Again, this is based somewhat on personal caprice, but let me give you an example of how I'd prioritize things. Some *A*'s would be: can opener, mixing bowls, paring knife, cookbooks (*A*'s only), wooden spoons, pancake turner, tongs, measuring equipment, trash container.

Some *B*'s would be: electric mixer, grater, aluminum foil, baking powder, food processor, salad oil, ricer.

Some *C*'s would be: cake decorating equipment, Jell-O molds, tapioca, custard cups, mallet, skewers, sieves, chafing dish.

I think examples are important for clarity, but they can be misleading so I want to caution you again. *My* food processor is a *B* to me. If you make your own baby food, let's say, then *your* food processor is definitely an *A*.

Another caution: Be honest with yourself. Don't kid yourself into thinking something is an *A* because your mother gave it to you. *A*'s are things you use more often than once a week. Without any given *A* you would experience a lot of inconvenience. It is hard to substitute something else for an *A* item.

My family, for instance, loves mashed potatoes, and without a potato masher it would be difficult to get the desired result and satisfy their appetites for mashed potatoes. On the other hand, without a cake-testing tool I could simply use a toothpick or a piece of spaghetti, or I could touch the center of the cake with my fingertips. In that case it's easy to improvise or do without a cake tester completely.

At the risk of straining my categorizing to the breaking point, remember:

A = vital (could hardly function without it)

B = important (inconvenient to function without it)

C = limited value, some value (could function without it if you had to)

D = complete waste (don't need it)

But if you're the type of person who carefully places the pencils in the drawer facing the same direction; if you could serve Beef Burgundy on the top of your hot water heater at any given moment; if you iron brown paper bags before placing them in descending order in the paper bag caddy, you're going to have some problems with this categorizing. For you it's going to be like trying to pick out your favorite noodle at a spaghetti dinner. You're going to pick up the Bisquick and agonize over whether it's an *A* or *B*. Heaven forbid you should make a mistake and misjudge it.

If you're suffering from Manic Perfectionist's Syndrome (MPS—not to be confused with PMS) here's Plan II. All you need to do is differentiate between *A*'s and *C*'s. Put all the *A*'s and *B*'s in one category and *C*'s in another. *C*'s seem to be somewhat more obvious than *A*'s and *B*'s, thus they're easier to categorize. See if Plan II isn't just the impetus you need to keep the **C-C-C**'s from becoming zzzzzzz's.

Now is a good time to stop. What lies ahead is a good day's work and you'll want to be refreshed and ready to go. For the rest of the day you'll need to operate the mixing center out of the categorized boxes, unless, of course, you quickly load the paraphernalia into the empty cupboards. If you opt for this method be sure to keep everything grouped, at least, into *A-B-C* category. Either way you'll be running the kitchen in a somewhat haphazard manner; but at least it won't look like an area worthy of being measured on the Richter scale.

C-ING IS BELIEVING

You've come a long way, baby, as they say, and now the end is in sight. What remains is my favorite part of the whole **C-C-C** process. Here's the grand finale: categorizing spaces and organizing the mixing center.

Take a close look at your mixing center and decide where all your *A* (or *A* and *B*) spaces are. Where will you stow *C*'s? Again, if you're an average-sized person, *A* and *B*'s are the top two drawers in a base cupboard and front half of top two overhead cupboards. The front half of a top base cupboard shelf would also be an *A* or *B*.

All you have to do now is to put the *A* and *B* gadgets into *A* and *B* places and put the *C* things in those areas which require steps, stretches, step-stools, or bending to reach. It's okay to move things out of the way in order to reach them, too. It's also acceptable (and sometimes necessary) to store mixing center *C*'s in an area

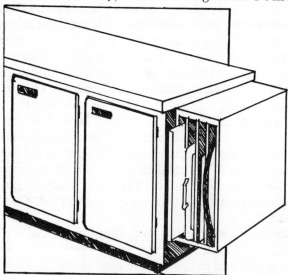

Stretch a base cupboard by attaching a tray or baking pan holder to the end.

other than the mixing center. The main thing is to make those *A*'s and *B*'s as handy as your space will allow.

If you're strapped for time, here's how to subdivide the whole **C-C-C** project. With some careful planning you can break down this clean, cull, categorize routine into micro pieces. Naturally, it'll take longer before you realize the final result, but you'll be able to get out of the kitchen without a court order.

Here's a plan of attack: **C-C-C** the base cupboards and drawers, then **C-C-C** the overhead storage areas. Or **C-C-C**, the gadgets and their storage areas, then **C-C-C** the food and its storage area.

Or try this. After you've personalized the mixing center list, adding and subtracting all the variables, prioritize the items on your list into *A-B-C* categories (or *A* and *C* categories if you're a victim of MPS). Then categorize your mixing center cupboards, drawers, and shelves into *A-B-C* areas and decide which *A* things will go into which *A* spaces and so on. In other words, the mixing center will be carefully planned before you actually *do* anything. With such organized premeditation you'll be able to **C-C-C** one drawer at a time, one shelf at a time, one cupboard at a time.

STARTING OVER

Following the timetable at the end of this chapter, you can now organize your entire kitchen, using the **C-C-C** approach. The mixing center rules you have just read are the standard **C-C-C** procedure for every center you set up. Just substitute "sink center" or "cooking center" when "mixing center" appears. Should you have enough kitchen space or a particular need for a refrigerator center or a serving center, you may include those areas as well.

The biggest problem you're likely to uncover will be with food. If you have reserve supplies it will be impossible to store it all in the various centers. In that case, here are a few options.

- Keep just a week's worth of supplies or your "use-all-the-time" staples (whatever your space permits) in the centers and the rest in the pantry, a less convenient cupboard, or other storage area.

- After you do your marketing, place the food required for the week's menus in the various centers and store the other items in a separate location.

- Some people like to shop at home. Here's what I mean: if you've got a freezer full of meat, fruits, and vegetables, and a pantry stocked with canned, bottled, and boxed goods, you can plan your menus for a week or two and pull all the necessary food items from their storage areas. Then store them for your immediate convenience in the various centers.

- If you have a pantry or large chef's cupboard where a stockpile of food and other supplies is kept, it's best not to include this area when you **C-C-C**. After you've **C-C-C**'d the gadgets and other equipment for each center, see if there's enough room for at least the *A* food items, and pull those things from the pantry.

Remember that the ideal is seldom a reality. You are bound to some degree by the physical structure of your kitchen. But aside from what appears to be an architectural plot against us, we can alter, to some degree at least, the speed and efficiency of KP duty.

I have taught this concept to thousands of women (and even a few men). They have come up with some very helpful and practical solutions, especially when elbow room is pretty much restricted to the periphery of the ribs.

One woman went so far as to categorize her spices: cinnamon, oregano, and chili powder were *A*'s. Saffron, turmeric, and fenugreek were *C*'s. So she alphabetized the *A*'s and put them in the front of her spice drawer and put the *C*'s in a less handy location. This left a lot of room in the drawer for more important and oft-needed items.

Another woman made homemade suckers about every three months or so and her mixing center was crammed with specialty bottles of flavorings. When she removed the extracts and stored them in a *C* location with the sucker molds, sticks, and labels, and wrappers, she made her mixing center not only more spacious but much more functional on a day-to-day basis.

Like many folks, I have a bouquet of tools sitting in a crock on the counter of my cooking center. It holds the wire whip, wooden spoons, and spatulas that I use every single day so one-motion storage is vital. Also, this crock arrangement frees up already limited drawer space.

An ambitious mother of three converted her front hall closet into a pantry complete with adjustable shelves. When the closet functioned as such, she considered it a *C* because it was always

Fliptop cupboard doors over the refrigerator make the contents more accessible. A basket provides extra storage.

used to stash junk. And, when guests came over, all their coats were put on someone's bed, anyway. So by converting the space into a food storage area—which, by the way, was only a few feet from the kitchen—she gained several square feet of *B* and *C* type storage.

ON THE LOOKOUT

If your new kitchen system is a drastic change from your old method, give the area a chance to work. You may experience a little frustration for a week or two until you feel comfortable with the locations of your necessities. Keep working with it and you'll begin to see your escape plans unfold.

If, however, you notice snags in a particular and often repeated operation, say making waffles, salad, or sandwiches, see if you can determine why the snafu is occurring. Here's a checklist of possible causes:

1. Are things being stored at the point of (most often) first use?

2. If so, do you need duplicates? Dupes are especially helpful when centers are several steps away from each other or totally isolated. Space permitting, it's usually wise to have twins of measuring spoons and cups, can/bottle openers, stirring spoons, pancake turners, mixing bowls, and salt and pepper shakers.

3. Do cupboards, drawer dividers, shelves or gadgets need to be labeled? This can save hours of nagging and keeps you from having to remember where everything is supposed to go.

4. Did you categorize something as a *C* or *D* that is actually a *B*?

If you've ever tried to fix your own plumbing, tune up the car, or get the garage door back in the track, you know that it takes three and one-half hours longer than if a professional were to handle the job. (Not to mention the $500 increase in cash outlay for emergency room charges!) Aside from more experience and perhaps know-how, the pros have the tools to do the job. If we had the specialty equipment Mr. Goodwrench has, we could rotate the tires in twelve minutes, too.

My point is this: It's possible to pare down your belongings to the point of gross inconvenience.

When I first got my mixer/food processor/blender I decided, purely for aesthetics, not to keep it on the kitchen counter. The only other available place was down the hall in the linen closet. Surely, I thought, I'd have enough self-discipline coupled with the desire to use my new toy to walk down the hall and cart it to the kitchen whenever I had a need for it. WRONG. Every time I had to grate, knead, or blend something I'd just say to myself, "It's easier to do it by hand than it is to lug that food processor into the kitchen." Within two weeks, after I realized my error, the machine was sitting in a corner on the counter.

While it *is* smart to rid your counters of all unnecessary apparatus and decorations, be sure you don't do it to a point where things become awkward and more difficult than they need to be.

Here's an approximate timetable to follow, set up to guide you through a complete kitchen overhaul in just three or four weeks. Sure, you can work at it faster if you have the endurance of a weight lifter, the determination of a black belt bargain hunter, and the patience of a Slurpee clerk at the 7-11. On the other hand, if you work outside the home, if you've got preschoolers, or if you just plain can't stand the thought of the undertaking (pun intended), give yourself two weeks for each designated week.

Whatever timetable you choose, here's the upshot in abbreviated fashion: **C-C-C** ASAP! **CCC**ing is just the ticket for an abbreviated tour of duty!

TIMETABLE

WEEK ONE

Monday	Plan simple menus for at least two weeks. Shop for ingredients. Group nonperishables in a box or other central location. Do whatever advance food preparation is possible for this week's menus (i.e., brown hamburger and freeze in serving portions; mix meatloaf or form meatballs and freeze; grate cheese, set a salad; make up a spice mix, etc.)
Tuesday-Saturday	Discard and sort. Go through entire kitchen using the four-box method.
Sunday:	Your day off.

WEEK TWO

Monday	Plan location of mixing center, cooking center, and sink center. Again, do whatever advance food preparation is possible for this week's menus.
Tuesday-Saturday	C-C-C the mixing center.
Sunday	Your day off.

WEEK THREE

Monday-Saturday	C-C-C the cooking center, sink center, and clean the refrigerator (if you're not setting up a refrigerator center).
Sunday	Your day off. (Bless your heart—you deserve it!)

WEEK FOUR

Monday-Saturday	C-C-C the refrigerator center and the serving center.

chapter 5

A KITCHEN TO SERVE YOU RIGHT

If reading the foregoing chapter made you feel like you've just gone nine rounds with King Kong Bundy and you haven't the strength for even one step-over toehold, don't give up and toss your sweat socks into the ring. The hard part is over and before long, you'll be declared the official winner.

Now that you've soaked up the knowledge and you're familiar with the plan, you're ready for some high-powered ideas that will wreak the final blow. Once and for all let's put an end to kitchen waste: wasted time, wasted space, and wasted energy (yours, in particular).

If you're working in a severely cramped or poorly designed kitchen, you may have to summon up some creativity to help you get the job done.

Here's what I mean. We are all bound to some degree by the architecture of our kitchens. For example, the measuring spoons, rubber spatula, gravy ladle, and potato peeler may seem best suited to drawer storage, but when you have no drawer space, start using your imagination.

Here's how: Think of the four storage alternatives. No matter how commodious or circumscribed your kitchen, there are only four ways to store things: hang them up, store them in a drawer, set them on a shelf, or put them on the floor.

No drawers for silverware? Store it on a shelf or countertop.

Make a simple knife rack out of scrap wood and attach it to a wall or cupboard base.

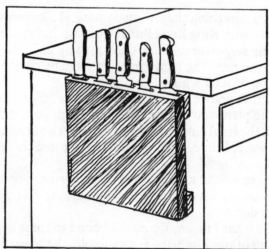

So, if drawer storage is not possible, ask yourself if those tools can be hung up, put on a shelf, or stored on the floor in some manner.

Whatever storage problem you are faced with, you can find your best storage alternative by looking at these four possibilities. Frequently, you can work around the existing architecture of your kitchen and save the many hours and dollars of a remodeling project.

HANG IT ALL

Keep knives and scissors within easy reach with a magnetic rack.

What can you hang up? Mops, brooms, ironing board, vacuum hose, bag of attachments, spice racks, pocketed shoe bags to hold cans of cleaners, etc., pails of supplies, pots and pans, cooking tools, and knives (on a magnetic holder or wooden form). Even bags of food like potato chips, powdered sugar, marshmallows, can be hung up. Just fold over the end of the bag, clamp it shut with a spring-paper clamp, and hang it up. You can also hang placemats using a spring action clamp.

Your garbage can hang up too, by using a garbage bag caddy. This organizer attaches to the inside of a sink cabinet door and is made to hold either plain paper bags or plastic trash bags. There are also hanging racks made to hold paper sacks and boxes of foil and plastic wrap.

Pan racks, mounted underneath a deep shelf, slide out to reveal hooks on which to hang pots and pans. Cups, mugs, measuring equipment, and any number of gadgets can likewise be hung on revolving or slide-out cup racks. Black wrought iron pan racks are

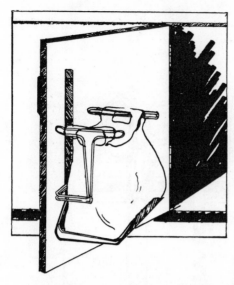

Want your trash easy to reach and out of sight? Hang a garbage bag caddy inside a cupboard door.

easily installed on a bit of wall or ceiling space.

Where can you hang things up? On a wall, inside a cupboard or closet door, high up under a sink, on a grid or pegboard, behind a door, or on any sturdy vertical surface. Grids are widely available, or you can make your own. Arrange seven 1x2's horizontally over three 1x2-inch vertical slats. Nail slats in place, paint, and hang equipment on the slats with hooks.

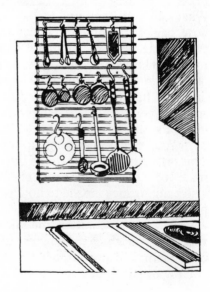

A grid hanging in the cooking or mixing center provides one-motion storage (especially handy when drawer space is limited).

Another hanging grid is made by simply attaching a piece of latticework to the wall or ceiling.

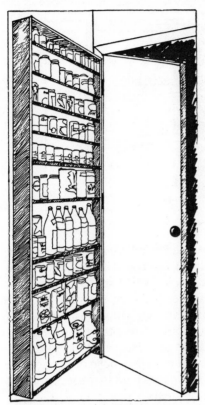

For extra storage, build a narrow shelf behind a kitchen door.

Hang a vinyl-dipped steel shelf inside a closet door.

Don't have enough shelf space? There are small vinyl-dipped steel shelves that can stand on an existing shelf, thus doubling your horizontal surface. There are bins that slide under and hang from an existing shelf, again utilizing wasted space. Many varieties of shelving units hang over a closet door or on the wall behind a door.

Plastic freezer containers, small sturdy cardboard boxes, or small purchased racks can be tacked to the inside of cupboard doors to hold spices, envelope packets, gelatin, and other lightweight items.

Small shelf units can be attached to the inside of cupboard doors.

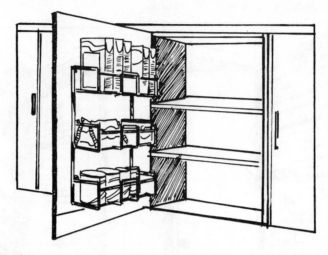

Look up! Shelves for seldom-used articles can be added above a door—or anywhere about two feet from the ceiling. They can be made inexpensively, using particle board supported by angle irons. That way you can free up your cabinet space for everyday utensils in constant demand. Also, if you have two cupboards with a window or a door interrupting them, a bridge over the top of the two units provides a shelf for decorative or infrequently used things. But this is only recommended if you're in dire need of extra space. The things stored on these high shelves are hard to retrieve and the shelves themselves are difficult to clean.

For the do-it-yourselfer a hanging storage unit can be made using only a screwdriver. Standard-sized shelves (8 in. x 24 in. seems just the right size) made from particle board form the shelves and uprights. Paint or stain and glue together. T-plates are positioned for support. (See illustration.)

Large and small, single- and double-tiered lazy Susans are readily available and beloved by many. They waste space, so proceed with caution, but they *are* extremely useful in cupboards with dead corners that are hard to reach.

No drawers? Without enough drawer space, you have to rely heavily on the other storage alternatives. But you can purchase drawers that mount (using only a screwdriver) under an upper cupboard unit or under any high horizontal surface. Freestanding drawer units made from wood, metal, cardboard, or plastic can sup-

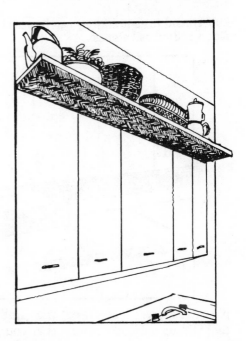

For extra C-type storage, build a shelf over a bank of cupboards.

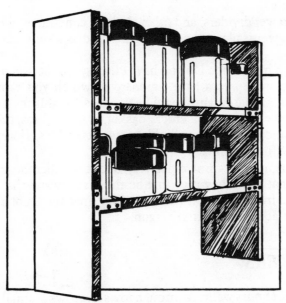

A simple, freestanding shelf made from scrap lumber and T brackets provides extra storage right where you need it.

Rubbermaid instant drawers can be attached under cupboards for extra gadget and utensil storage.

ply extra drawer space. (Keep the cardboard away from fire and water.) Sliding shallow drawers that you install on any base cabinet shelf are also available.

Dishpans, drawer dividers, and other shallow containers can function like a drawer if placed on a shelf and used as a slide-out tray.

Every kitchen has a floor. Do you have clean spaces between the refrigerator or stove and a base cupboard in which you can stand serving trays, a large cutting board, or cookie sheets? Is there a corner where you could stand a crock, basket, stacking bins, or other large containers? These can hold fruits, vegetables, flour, sugar, baking pans, or anything.

Use your imagination, think creatively, and remember those four storage alternatives. They may just be the magic wand that turns your kitchen from a pumpkin into a luxury liner and if not a luxury liner, then at least a station wagon.

SPACE MAKERS

A while back I spent hours walking through rows and rows of small kitchen appliances. I was delighted to see the panoply. Manufacturers are giving us the convenience we so desperately need but not, as in times past, at the expense of counter-top space. The new surge of interest is in space-saving appliances that are installed on overhead cupboards, so you don't have to play checkers with your equipment come supper time.

One of my favorites is the blender/can opener made by Waring. Like the other space makers it mounts under a cabinet and flips in such a way as to expose the blender or electric can opener, whichever is needed.

Another dandy is a complete mixer storage unit made by Black and Decker. The under-the-cabinet unit houses a portable mixer, beaters, and power cord.

There are many varieties of coffee makers (some with clocks, automatic timers, and measure markings); can openers (some open screw-top jars, bottles, and slit bags, and have removable cutting assemblies for ease in cleaning); and radios (complete with clocks, cassette players, and automatic timers).

Another small appliance called a Broil-R-Ange performs many heating and cooking functions. Covering a space only 20 in. long, $8\frac{1}{2}$ in. deep, and 4 in. high, this device heats, broils, warms, defrosts, fries, and toasts. The appliance has a 5 in. electric cooking element in addition to one that broils meat, toasts or grills sandwiches, warms liquids, or defrosts frozen food. This "do it all" implement is especially helpful in apartments and dorms, though it could also put a mini cooking center closer to your sink, if the main cooking center is located in a remote spot.

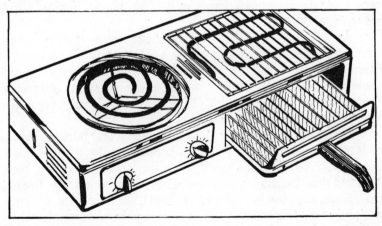

Small appliances like the Broil-R-Ange are well-suited to small apartments. They can also provide a mini cooking center wherever you need it.

Most of these appliances appear easy to clean and some manufacturers even advertise that the equipment is resistant to steam, grease, and cooking vapors.

If you've always wanted the convenience of electric appliances but never had the space, take a trip to your favorite neighborhood store and see for yourself the array of space makers available.

Here We Go Again

I know. All I do is harp, harp, harp. But the best way to gain more space is to rid yourself of *C*'s and *D*'s.

I have a *C* box in my kitchen; you can have one in each center if you need to. My *C* box is a large square plastic container (I don't use the lid) that sits on a high C-type shelf. In this box are a wide variety of *C* items that I use from time to time: corn on the cob holders, the pouring lid from a shake and pour glass, extra measuring equipment, spare can opener, skewers, donut cutter, garlic press (now you know I'm not exactly gourmet caliber), turkey baster, melon baller, funnel. When I need something from the box I slide it down off the shelf and select the needed tool. I use these things so infrequently that the few seconds spent rummaging are a small price to pay for freed-up space.

Cookie cutters and cake-decorating tools are boxed separately in plastic containers (with lids) so I can stack them up. If you have a large cookie-cutter collection, separate them by holiday or season and package in separate smaller boxes and don't forget to label them accordingly.

Another way to reduce the amount of storage space you need is to hang things decoratively on the kitchen wall. This is especially effective with baskets (remember my bamboo steamer?), molds, cookware, ladles, anything . . . as long as it's pretty and interesting. Hang it up. It's still accessible while contributing valuable usage/ storage space to those vital *A*'s.

I can nag until I sound like a wounded water buffalo, but the odds are against me, I know. Most of you are still going to stack up those brown paper sacks. You'll shake the crumbs from your bread bags and stuff them into a drawer. Cool-Whip containers, frosting, margarine, and chip dip tubs, coffee and Crisco cans are just going to seduce you and you'll quail at the thought of discarding them. (World-class junkaholics will experience the same sensations regarding cottage cheese and yogurt containers.)

What to do? Control yourself! Designate *one* container or *one* area of space to house these addicting objects and when that spot is filled, start tossing (or immediately give away) the rest. When your collection begins to dwindle, start stocking up again. Just don't exceed your boundaries.

Sub for Space

Instead of buying pans and dishes in every conceivable size, try substituting. *Better Homes and Gardens* suggests the following alternatives:

An 8 in. x 1½ in. round pan holds approximately 1½ quarts. *Use: 10 in. x 6 in. x 2 in. dish, 9 in. x 1½ in. round pan, 8 in. x 4 in. x 2 in. loaf pan, or 9 in. pie plate.*

An 8 in. x 8 in. x 2 in. square pan holds approximately 2 quarts. *Use: 11 in. x 7 in. x 1½ in. pan, 12 in. x 7½ in. x 2 in. pan, 9 in. x 5 in. x 3 in. loaf pan, or two 8 in. x 1½ in round pans.*

A 13 in. x 9 in. x 2 in. pan holds approximately 3 quarts. *Use: 14 in. x 11 in. x 2 in. baking dish, two 9 x 1½ in. round pans, or three 8 in. x 1½ in. round pans.*

To determine if one pan can be substituted for another, fill them with water and measure each. If the volume is similar, substituting is okay. However, you may need to adjust baking times. (This will depend on the size of the dish used and the depth of the food.)

If the substitute pan is deeper than the size recommended in the recipe, increase the baking time. Conversely, shallower pans require shortened baking times. In any case, be sure to test for doneness according to the recipe directions.

When substituting glass for metal, reduce the baking temperature 25 degrees. You may also need to reduce the baking time.

PHYSICALLY FIT

It seems impossible to physically fit together the odd mix of packages you need to store; i.e., boxes, bags, bottles, and cans. The varying shapes often force you to store unlike items behind or on top of each other. With this arrangement, one-motion storage is virtually impossible, never mind keeping things in *A-B-C* priority order.

The solution is simple: square plastic freezer containers. I have transferred all our dry food (baking powder, baking soda, corn starch, corn meal, tapioca, biscuit mix, oatmeal, pasta, sugar, flour, etc.) into these inexpensive but durable containers. They come in all different sizes: tall ones are good for shelves with an expanse of vertical space between them; wide, squat containers are perfect for horizontal areas. The smallish, plastic freezer boxes are perfect for baking soda, baking powder, corn starch, tapioca, and homemade spice mixes (see *Confessions of an Organized Housewife* for recipes). All sizes combined work together to eat up every square inch of available space while allowing you to see at a glance everything the cupboard contains.

I label the boxes with masking tape and felt marker, then when I want to change a container's ingredients, it's easy to remove the old label and make a new one. Also, directions (for making oatmeal, pancakes, or cornmeal muffins) are cut from the original box and dropped into the freezer container or, tape them to the lid or side of the container.

Being similar in shape, the boxes fit together like puzzle pieces. You can stack them (*A*'s on top) or put two uniform-sized containers one behind the other, *A*'s in front. There are other advantages: because the lids close securely the food stays fresher and pests and excess moisture are discouraged. The food is also easier to measure after all, it's no small task trying to measure ½ cup of cocoa from a cocoa can!

Drawer dividers help my centers stay on track. I use standard drawer dividers in my gadget drawer so I can grab tongs, spatula, or paring knife with one motion. A large plastic container (made for holding a large loaf of bread) serves as a "file" for pan lids. I slide it out, grab the needed lid, and slide the container back. (Ditto with Tupperware lids.)

A drawer divider sits on a shelf to corral bottles of extracts and flavorings, which are labeled around the neckband with masking tape and felt markers. Another drawer divider serves as a "file" for envelopes and flavoring packets.

To keep drawer dividers from sliding around when you open the drawer, place cardboard tubes from paper towels or bathroom tissue in the back of the drawer; they can be cut to fit and the dividers are easily removed for cleaning. Floral clay or carpet tape, which is tacky on both sides, can also be used and still allow the dividers to be removed for cleaning. Just be sure to use plenty of drawer dividers.

SPICY INFO

Spices pose a common storage problem. There are, of course, commercial spice racks you can purchase. Some are decorative to hang on a kitchen wall. This type usually requires that you transfer purchased spices from the original package into the decorative bottles that come with the spice rack. These organizers are okay, but I've discovered that any jar sitting out in a kitchen gets coated with a "caterpillar fuzz" of airborne grease and dust, making frequent soap and water clean-ups necessary. This problem is compounded when the spice rack is hung by the stove. For these reasons, I've chosen other spice storage options. But, don't grieve if you have to use a standard spice rack. They *do* have a few advantages: they're easily mounted wherever you need them and they offer up one-motion storage. The cleaning problem is the only downside.

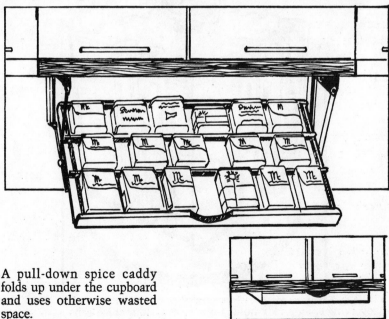

A pull-down spice caddy folds up under the cupboard and uses otherwise wasted space.

My favorite method is to keep the spices in a drawer. I label the tops of the cans with permanent felt marker and put the spices in alphabetical order.

I frequently purchase large bottles of things like dried parsley, cinnamon, peppercorns, etc., and they're too big for the spice drawer. So, I label the lids of the spice jars and put these oversized containers in a deep square plastic freezer container. This box then serves as a drawer or slide-out tray on a base cupboard shelf.

Another option is to store the large bottles in a *C*-location and use them occasionally to refill the small containers that can be stored more conveniently.

Spices can be organized and contained in small boxes or plastic drawer dividers fitted to size. (Velveta cheese boxes are just the right size.) Vinyl-coated wire spice racks are available at many discount and variety stores and are often found in mail order catalogs. These spice caddies are mounted, by using only a screwdriver, to the inside of a cupboard door. Since there are always a few inches of wasted space on the front of overhead shelves anyway, using available (and out of sight) door storage is a good way to eliminate any barren square inches.

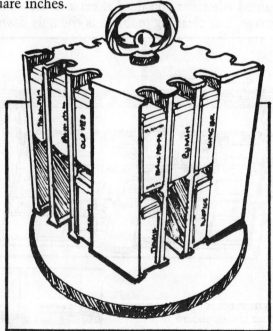

A revolving spice caddy holds up to twenty-four spice cans.

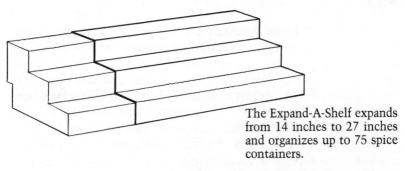

The Expand-A-Shelf expands from 14 inches to 27 inches and organizes up to 75 spice containers.

If your spice cupboard looks like this . . .

it can look like this with an Expand-A-Shelf

A revolving square spice caddy has an advantage over turntables or lazy Susans. It holds twenty-four spice cans and the square design eliminates wasted space. Each can's label is completely visible, and because the can is contained *inside* the spice rack, the cans don't fall or slide off when the gadget is rotated (unlike lazy Susans).

A dandy stairstep invention called Expand-A-Shelf puts up to seventy-five spice containers in full view great for one-motion storage. The three "stairs" expand from 14 in. to 27 in. to hold cans of soup, small jars or cans of food, medicine, or vitamins. And that's just in the kitchen!

The Expand-A-Shelf and other organizing products are available by mail order from the Idea Center, P.O. Box 492, Bountiful, UT 84010.

Nowadays, many kitchens come complete with a built-in spice storage cupboard that's mounted on the front of a cupboard door. These are extremely useful, as well as attractive, since the spices are stored one layer deep. The only drawback is once in a while the builder or kitchen designer will install the specialty cupboard in an odd or out-of-the-way location. If this is the case in your kitchen and you find yourself setting off on a search and rescue mission every time you need the fennel seed, store the *A*'s and/or *B*'s in a more accessible location and use the built-in for reserve supplies or *C* spice storage. If you don't have to worry about youngsters, you can use these customized spice cupboards for vitamins, medicine, or any other objects that will fit on the narrow shelves.

OUT OF THE CUPBOARD

While we're on the subject of built-in specialty cabinets, two common ones come to mind. Many newer homes have a deep cupboard over the refrigerator with vertical dividers. These are designed to hold baking pans and trays. Baking pans, you'll remember, should actually be stored in the mixing center. Trays should be stored in the serving center or close to the dishes, at least.

A deep divided cupboard over the refrigerator is handy for trays and baking pans.

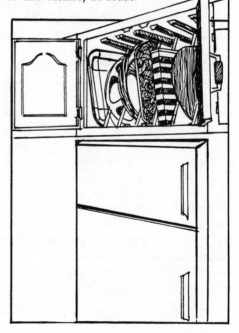

These over-the-refrigerator cupboards are so useful that I don't mind the occasional dislocation, as it were. Because they're deep, they're much more accessible than their 12 in. deep predecessors. Besides, whenever I'm making something that requires a baking pan, I usually need a refrigerated item anyway. So, I grab the pan when I go to the refrigerator.

As for trays, no one in our house is served breakfast in bed and we use trays primarily when I'm entertaining. So, I've decided they're *C*'s, and over the refrigerator is a perfect place for a *C*.

Another commonly seen built-in is the deep narrow drawer designed, again, for trays and cookie sheets. These are typically installed in U-shaped kitchens in one of the corners (instead of those awkward and hard-to-reach dead corner shelves or turntables—i.e., outer darkness) My attitude toward these organizers is pretty much the same as above. Cookie sheets and trays are *B*'s or *C*'s anyway. So, if they're not located in the correct center, it's no big deal.

What I'm hoping you'll glean from all this philosophy is that frequently you have to work around your existing architecture. If that is painfully inconvenient, think creatively. "What else can I put into that unit besides baking pans and trays?" For example, if the deep, narrow cookie sheet or tray drawer is by the sink, you could install a towel rack for wet dishcloths, dish towels, and rubber gloves, and/or a paper towel holder. A deep bread drawer can easily be used as a file drawer for anything from receipts to recipes.

A deep bread drawer can be converted into a file drawer.

GENERIC ADVICE FOR SPECIFIC PROBLEMS

If you have a bank of deep shelves somewhere in your kitchen (making your reserve supplies difficult to see and retrieve) there are a few things you can do to make this glorious storage space more commodious. Shallow cardboard boxes can serve as slide-out trays. Install Rubbermaid pull-out shelves. Half-shelves made from vinyl coated steel help eliminate wasted space. Store canned goods in "grocery aisles" with three inches or so between rows. That way you can store unlike items behind each other, yet you'll still be able to see and select the right ingredient. Place soup cans into a juice can dispenser (originally designed for freezer use) and they roll right out.

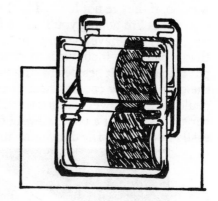

Soup cans can be organized in a juice can dispenser.

Deep shelves, particularly those used for food storage, need to be straightened regularly. (I spend about five minutes a month on my pantry and it never gets too far out of control.) So, use some of the previously mentioned organizational ideas and straighten your deep shelves regularly, and you'll get good quality service from these storage areas.

Another common problem is the "dead corner" kitchen cupboard (better known as the Phantom Zone, Bermuda Triangle, or Chamber of Horrors). If your kitchen is quite storage worthy, use the dead corner to hold *C*'s (preferably large ones). Smaller stored items should be housed in some type of container so they can be moved as one unit. If you desperately need the space, put the *A*'s and *B*'s in front and the *C*'s in back.

A turntable installed in a corner base cupboard eliminates dead storage space.

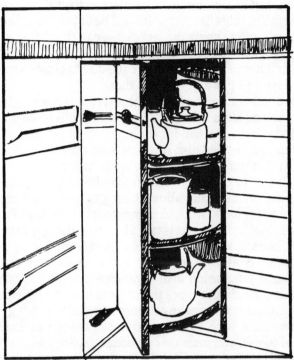

If the corner has a built-in turntable it will function more effectively if you straighten it periodically. Some of these turntables aren't overly sturdy, so if that's the case, use it for lightweight storage: cereal, plastic refrigerator containers, boxes of food, pasta, etc.

To keep the turntable organized, shallow boxes can be used to corral and categorize various foods—soup in one box, cake mixes in another, and so on. Since the lazy Susan is round and the boxes are square you'll waste a little space this way, but if time is more valuable to you than space, the waste of the latter is okay.

If you're up to a little remodeling, check Chapter 12, "By Design," for some great corner cupboard projects.

SERVES YOU RIGHT

It's a toss up where you store your dishes. If you use two sets (one for breakfast, lunch, and snacks, and another for dinner) it may work well to store the former close to the snack bar, cooking center, or mixing center, provided you serve food to the individual plates immediately after preparation. The dinnerware, then, can be stored in a hutch or china cabinet or close to the dining room table.

If you use one set of dishes (as I do) except for special occasions, I find it most helpful to store the dishes close to the sink, so they're easier to put away after a meal.

For quicker clean-up use a dishpan to cart dishes, glasses, and flatware to and from the table. That way you'll be able to set and clear the table in one trip for each.

There are myriad dish organizers on the market and I might add many of them do indeed save space and provide one motion storage. If you've got more vertical than horizontal space between shelves, the dividers that allow the plates and bowls to stand on edge (like file folders) work extremely well. I couldn't keep house without mine! If your space is more horizontal, there are units that function like stacking in/out baskets. And combination of the two types enables you to squeeze out every square inch of potential space! When purchasing dish organizers it's best to buy several small units of different types than it is to buy one large piece. The smaller dividers give you much more versatility.

Organizers with built-in cup hooks are not as versatile, are awkward to use, and increase cup breakage. So, look out for them. Secondhand stores are full of these organizers which leads me to believe my theory is right!

That's a Switch!

For a refreshing change I'm going to tell you how you can *get* things instead of how to get rid of them! If you're down to three goblets, two cups (I bet you still have eight saucers), and five dinner plates (two of them chipped), here's a ray of hope. Check with your local department store, bridal registry, or china shop and see if your pattern has been discontinued. If not, order the pieces you need and get your set back in honeymoon condition.

If you find, however, that your pattern is an endangered species you will probably be money ahead by selling or donating your leftovers. Then, start from scratch with a new design.

If your discontinued set is missing only a few pieces, though, here's help. In *Woman's Day* magazine (May 21, 1985, page 20) they published a list of companies that specialize in odd pieces from discontinued china and crystal patterns.

Woman's Day recommends you send a self-addressed stamped envelope to the manufacturer with as much information as you can scrape (that's plate talk) together (i.e., pattern name, number, color, etc.). If that information has been scoured from the bottom of the china or crystal, take a close-up photo and send that.

THE BLUE PLATE
ANTIQUES
Box 31205
Raleigh, NC 27622

CHINA MATCH
9 Elmford Road
Rochester, NY 14606

FRAN JAY/POPCORN
Box 1057
Fleminston, NJ 08822

THE JEWEL BOX
Box 145
Albertville, AL 35950

JUDY'S HOUSE OF HOPE
2968 Appling Drive
Chamblee, GA 30341

LOCATOR'S INC.
908 Rock Street
Little Rock, AR 72202

PATTERNS UNLIMITED
Box 15238
Seattle, WA 98115

REPLACEMENTS, LTD.
1510 Holbrook Street
Greensboro, NC 27403

TABLETOP MATCHING
SERVICE
Box 205
Cookeville, TN 38501

SOS FOR THE SERVING CENTER

Wherever you choose to store the dishes, it's smart to keep the serving center food close by. On the serving center list you'll notice that this is the type of food usually served the way it is, directly to the plates: potato chips, cookies, prepared cereals, crackers, etc. You know. All the fattening, insalubrious, carcinogenic stuff.

Notorious in this category are potato chip bags (which always seem to rip open down the middle of the bag); cellophane cookie bags (ditto); and the bane of motherhood—cereal boxes.

Escape from the Kitchen

When I open the Cheerios, I unfold the waxed lining with the precision of a neurosurgeon. But not the kids. It's rip open the box, tear out the lining, and go for the pack of super-sonic bubble gum (that glows in the dark) lying in what's left of the box. Have you ever tried to pour cereal into a bowl that's just been declared officially decimated? What results is four or five Lucky Charms in the bowl and three or four hundred on the table, floor, and in the lap of the pourer.

Needless to say, the serving center needs help. The first thing I did was to enforce this hard and fast rule: open cereal boxes perfectly. (That's about the only rule that stands with any degree of consistency around our house.)

When we buy the low-budget cereal that comes in a plastic bag, I transfer it into an empty cereal box and label it accordingly. Bags of food—cereal, marshmallows, chips, etc—can also be hung up by using a spring action paper clamp. Clip the bag shut and hang it up on any vertical surface.

Rubbermaid and Tupperware make squarish pouring containers that are handy for storing cereal. Action industries makes several useful (and very inexpensive) plastic storage containers. My favorites (for holding serving center food) are the ones that hold $3^3/_4$ liter and $1^3/_4$ liter. They are squarish and look like large plastic jars with wide-mouth screw-top lids. The large size is ideal for holding chips, crackers, cereal, spaghetti, lasagne, staples, etc. The smaller container holds marshmallows, raisins, pretzels, cookies, pasta, Cream of Wheat, corn meal, etc.

Label each container so everyone can plainly see what's inside. If you have base cupboards with pull-out shelves, that's the best place to keep serving center food stored in this manner. Just label the lids so you'll have a bird's eye view. And Rubbermaid makes a pull-out tray that's installed, using only a screw driver, onto stationary shelves, should you want to convert your space.

Also, Rubbermaid and Tupperware have see-through square storage containers, eliminating the need for labeling. They are, however, more expensive than brands like Action, Super Seal, and Freezette. Be sure to read the labels when you're selecting a container. Some will peel when exposed to hot foods and they may not be dishwasher safe.

Rubbermaid slide-out shelves make deep base cupboards more accessible.

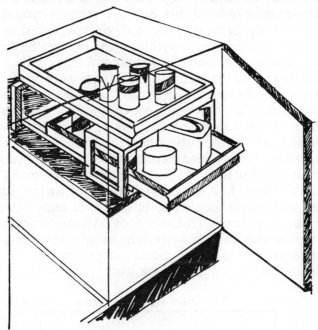

BABY, IT'S COLD INSIDE

Take a peek inside your refrigerator. Those *A-B-C*'s should be self-evident. Here's what I mean.

Everything in the refrigerator should have a well-defined, well-confined place. For example, the first shelf in our refrigerator is for dairy products and beverages. (The dairy products are *A*'s and the top shelf is an *A*.

The second shelf is used for leftover storage and things that need to be used up quickly: ground meat, fresh produce, lunch meat, etc. The third shelf holds two square plastic freezer containers without lids. The large container holds all the *B* and *C* bottles and jars: molasses, soy sauce, reserve bottle of catsup, buttermilk powder, lemon juice, kumquat preserves. The *A* bottles and jars and dispensers are stored handily with one-motion storage on the shallow door shelves.

The other container is about the size of a loaf of bread; it houses lunch meat and cold cuts. Both of these containers serve as drawers. We slide them out, make the selection, and slide them back in. This system keeps everything contained and the contents of the refrigerator are always fairly neat and organized.

The most space- and time-saving thing you can do with your refrigerator is to be sure the door opens the right way. It should open toward the adjacent counter, not away from it. Most refrigerators sold today are two-way doors, making it easy to install the handle and door hinges on either side of the door. If your door opens the wrong way, it adds a good six or seven feet of walking distance every time you open it. So, if your refrigerator door is guilty, see if it's a changeable model and take care of that problem immediately.

The deep freeze should also be organized using freezer baskets or cardboard boxes. That way each category of food will be fenced into its own location. Sometimes a map of the freezer is necessary to speed up the search and seizure process.

Here's what a map might look like:

View from top: upper level

Basic Ground Beef	Roasts, Steaks	Main Dishes	
Chicken	Bread, Baked Goods	Veg.	Fruits

View from top: lower level

Pork & Ham	Bacon-Sausage	Ice Cream & Ice
Lamb	Wild Game	Novelties

*View of inside of
upright freezer*

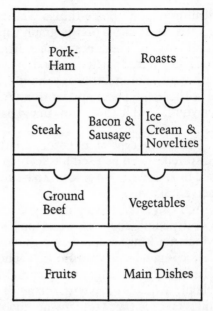

You can go one step further with freezer efficiency by keeping a perpetual freezer inventory sheet on a sheet of graph paper inside a kitchen cupboard door. On the left side of the sheet list, in alpha-

			1	2	3	4	5	6	7	8			
Bacon			✓	✓	✓	✗							
Basic G.B.			✓	✓	✓	✓	✓	✓	✓	✗			
Bread			✓	✓	✗								
Celery			✓	✓	✓	✓	✗						
Chicken			✓	✓	✓	✗							
Corn			✓	✗	✗								
Cube Steak			✓	✗									

betical order, list all the things you usually have in your freezer. The vertical columns on the graph paper are numbered along the top and bottom. Then, beside each listed item, check off the number on hand of that particular food. As you remove something from the freezer, make an X through the check mark, starting at the right side of the graph paper and working to the left as things are used. Then you'll be able to see how many packages of each category are left.

This same type of inventory chart is good for any things you have stored. It can be used for keeping a record of your home-preserved food. It will also give you a better idea of how much food to preserve next year.

You can increase the life of your chart by making the checks and x's in pencil. This way, when food is replaced, you can erase the previous markings and indicate the amount currently on hand.

Keeping tabs on your frozen cache is important. For that reason I keep my running inventory right in my calendar/planning notebook, which I have with me at all times. One newspaper columnist reported that I tote my notebook around much like a little girl clutches her Cabbage Patch Kid! I'll explain how to set up your own planning notebook in Chapter 9.

Using the form found on page 73 I always have a running list of the freezer's contents. If I'm in the store and I see an unadvertised special on pot roast, let's say, I just flip open my notebook and in an instant I know how many, if any, pot roasts I already have on hand. I can almost see your eyeballs rolling, but it's not as much trouble as it sounds. Keep a spiral notebook or some Post-it Notes and a pencil by the freezer. (Chain them to the wall if necessary.) Tell family members to write down anything they remove from the freezer. Then, before you do your shopping for the week, tear off the list and update your inventory.

Another method is to make up your week's menus, pull everything from the freezer that you'll need for the week, and store these foods in the kitchen refrigerator freezer. Mark the inventory at this time. That way the food will be handy come mealtime and you won't have to worry about whether someone remembered to mark off the chicken they pulled from the freezer.

Also, it's really only important to inventory *A* and *B* frozen goods.

HINTS FOR A
HASSLE-PROOF KITCHEN

- An ice cube bin holds approximately three dozen eggs and can be a great step saver if your cooking center and your refrigerator are yards apart. Just cart the ice cube bin to the desired center. This is a lot easier than trying to juggle a handful of eggs.

- If you make sandwiches very often, keep a tray (or square plastic freezer container) filled with all the necessary condiments. It's easier to grab a tray than individual bottles.

- Buy jelly in a squirt-type dispenser or transfer it into a clean catsup dispenser. Squirting the jelly eliminates the use of a knife so there are no more toast crumbs or pieces of butter or peanut butter floating around in the jelly.

- A shower cap is a great bowl cover, or can be used to cover cut watermelon. Or you can use one to cover the bowl you're whipping cream in. Punch the beaters through the shower cap, put the cap over the bowl and beat away with no splatters.

- A rubber band placed kitty-corner over the corners of the cutting board will keep it from slipping.

- A dampened sponge makes a good spoon rest, and you can wipe up spills as you go.

- Snap a plastic lid over the bottom of your flour sifter. This keeps your counter clean when you set it down. (I keep my sifter right inside the flour container.)

- Store a set of measuring spoons right by the spices. Toss a set into the spice drawer or hang them in the spice cabinet.

- Make new red markings on your plastic measuring cups by painting nail polish over the raised marking. When dry scrape off the markings and the red background will illuminate the measurement, making it easier to read.

- Use an old drip coffeepot to hold fat for deep frying. Pour the used fat into the pot—the strainer strains it. Clean out the strainer and store the coffeepot in the refrigerator. When deep frying again, heat the solidified fat right in the coffeepot and pour into your electric fry pan or deep saucepan. This eliminates the need for a space eating deep fryer.

- This isn't necessarily a kitchen tip, but it's a good one. Coffee filters are perfect for covering drainage holes in plant pots. Put the filter in the pot before you add the potting soil. The filter allows the water to drain from the plant but it keeps the dirt inside.

- Margarine containers, etc, are just the right size for individual servings of ice cream, pudding, Jell-O, leftovers, or what have you. That way you eliminate the mess people make when they want to dish up something. Be sure to label accordingly.

- I store cookies (three or four per serving) in sandwich baggies. It's a lot less mess than having the kids drag the whole bag of cookies around. Also, I have more control over how many cookies they eat.

- Color code your frozen food. Tie the beef with a red cord, pork with blue, and so on.

- Self-adhesive cork or carpet squares make great bulletin boards for shopping list, coupons, messages, freezer inventory, calendar, job charts, etc. If you want, keep them out of sight inside a cupboard door.

- Hang helpful charts inside your cupboard doors: equivalent measures, substitutions, calorie counter, freezing and roasting directions, metric conversion table, and often-used recipes.

- Heavy plastic floor runners make good shelf lining for pots, pans, and canned goods. Other options are self-adhesive floor tiles, oil cloth, vinyl, vinyl wallpaper, etc. When laying the self-adhesive type of shelf liner, cut off only a 1-inch border instead of peeling off the entire piece of backing. With only the periphery to adhere, it makes the paper much easier to work with.

- To keep nesting nonstick pans from scarring each other, separate them with paper toweling, a paper plate, or coffee filters.

- Keep a small can (or other container) for small unidentified objects you come across in your kitchen (screw, button, change, game piece, etc.). This catchall works fine as long as you periodically discard the long-standing dead wood. Also, no fair expanding this idea to two cans or three cans, or four cans or. . . .

- A pocketed shoe bag can be used to hold awkward gadgets, attachments for the food processor or vacuum, big spoons, ladles, tools, mail, receipts, bank statements, etc.
- To keep tablecloths creaseless, use an empty paper towel tube at the inside fold. Store in a drawer or hang tube and cloth over a hanger.
- To store plastic bags try one of these ideas. Stuff them inside a paper towel tube, canister, empty Crisco can (a bag saver would, of course, be a can saver) or an empty Boutique tissue box.
- Store small plastic tubs in a dishpan. Set the dishpan on a shelf and use it as a drawer.
- Sock sorters (plastic discs with an X slit in the middle) can be used as reusable plastic bag closures. Or, cut your own from extra plastic lids.
- Keep skewers in a plastic toothbrush container.
- An eyeglass case (open ended) or leather comb case provides safe storage for meat and candy thermometers.
- Store a used steel wool pad in an unglazed clay pot. The ultra-absorbent clay keeps the pad from rusting.
- When loading the dishwasher, fill it with all the small things first. If there's room for the big things, that's fine; if not it's better to wash a few large items than several small ones.
- Put a plastic pot scrubber in one section of the silverware basket in your dishwasher. This will keep the point of the paring knife, skewers, potato peeler, etc. from falling through.

Now that everything is humming along, all you have to do (especially until the family understands the program) is to maintain your centers with the fervor of the evangelist. Whenever you notice something out of place, quietly and quickly, return it to its designated home. This only takes a second or two—a far cry from what you've just been through.

Maintaining order is like keeping your money in the bank—the dividends just keep piling up; only *this* interest is paid with time.

chapter 6

THOUGHT FOR FOOD

Quick. For twenty points and Aunt Jemima's home phone number, give me one good reason why you should take the time to plan menus. If you're like most people I encounter, you frequently say things like, "Gee, I know I should plan menus, but I just don't have time." The reason you don't have time is because you haven't discovered just how *much* time planning menus saves you in the first place.

Since most of the work you do in your kitchen has to do with food, menu planning is the single most important contributing factor in your escape from the kitchen. Here are seven good reasons why:

1. **Good nutrition saves time.** Think about it. When you take five minutes a week to thoughtfully plan dinner menus (at least), you're more conscious of what you and your family are eating. Meals thrown together at the last minute usually fulfill just one requirement—satisfying hunger. You know that good nutrition helps you resist sickness, increases energy and stamina, and helps reduce stress. All of these things are tremendous time bandits, so, it only makes sense to eat right in the first place and avoid the pitfalls of insalubrious eating habits. Menu planning can be the first step in a sound nutritional program.

Menu planning also makes dieting easier. With a list of organized, low-calorie meals that's matched with the required ingredients, you'll be more likely to stick to your diet. Staying on top of your food preparations will motivate you to stay true to your diet instead of grabbing handfuls of chips, cookies, and candy. After all, you're going to eat whatever is lying around the house. So, plan for healthful meals and stock up on their nutritious ingredients.

With menu plans you're more conscious of: minimum daily food requirements; having enough to eat so you're not suffering from constant hunger; variety—so your desire for different tastes and textures is satisfied. A haphazard eat-on-the-run plan will center your eating habits on food fancies instead of food facts.

2. Menu planning helps you reduce the number of trips you make to the grocery store and/or your neighbor's house. How many times, when you're throwing dinner together at the eleventh hour, have you discovered (halfway into the meal) that you don't have a certain ingredient called for in the recipe you're whipping up? Too late to turn back, you run down to the store or over to the neighbor's to pick up the stray item. Don't kid yourself. These little detours are very costly in terms of time and often in terms of money, too.

When meals are planned in advance and a shopping list made out accordingly, there are no surprises, come mealtime—especially if you mark all necessary ingredients with a red signal dot so family members won't mistakenly gobble something up before its debut.

3. Menu planning saves money. Knowing your food requirements in advance helps you cash in on coupons, advertised sales, and savings due to in-season produce. Planning provides incorporation of leftovers so unnecessary waste is eliminated. With your menus planned and their ingredients handy, you spend less money on fast foods and restaurant meals.

4. Menu plans make the most out of what time you do have available. Check over your week's schedule and discover what time commitments are upcoming. On those nights when time is short you can plan nutritious, quick meals or simple meals the kids can put together.

I've discovered on the days I don't plan anything in particular, everyone fends for himself (instead of getting something ready for the entire family). Then we have several concurrent messes—none of which anyone feels responsible for—and before long the kitchen is totally out of control. A few minutes eliminates this time-costly scene.

5. With written menu plans you're more likely to delegate some

of your meal preparation responsibilities. Post the dinner menu and indicate which jobs are delegated to whom. This is especially helpful if you're not home when the kids come home from school. Someone can scrub the potatoes, put the meatloaf in the oven, and toss a salad, let's say. But if your meal plans are in your head, 100 percent of the work will be in *your* hands.

6. **Menu planning makes dovetailing possible.** What's dovetailing? It's doubling up your efforts—getting two for the price of one. It's starting dinner after breakfast so you'll have one cleanup instead of two. It's making three meat loaves instead of one. You're dovetailing when you make extra rice for tonight's stir-fry beef that will be used for tomorrow's rice pudding. (I'll give specific how-to's later in the chapter.)

7. **Menu planning relieves stress.** Procrastination is at the heart of a stressful life. (If not the heart, at least the pancreas.) We rush off to work or get busy around the house and put off the decision about what to fix for dinner. But as the day wears on, the harping in the mind's far periphery becomes louder and louder. "What shall I fix for dinner?"

Then when stomachs start to growl and hungry tempers flare, we're either seen standing by the stove scraping off the thawed outside portion of the hamburger or waiting in a long line of cars hoping that soon we'll hear those cheerful words, "Welcome to McDonald's. May I take your order, please?"

Menu planning enables you to decide *once* what to fix for dinner and eliminates facing the anxiety every day.

TRY IT, YOU'LL LIKE IT

Perhaps I've given you a little nudge in the right direction with all this sound, logical advice. But the real conversion will come after the trial of your faith, so to speak. What I'm really asking is that you'll give menu planning a try.

Have you ever noticed this sales pitch: "Examine this product free for ten days. If you're not completely satisfied, just send it back and you'll be under no obligation." Well, try that with menu planning. Just give it a shot for ten days and see what a difference it makes! You will feel so unburdened, almost lighthearted. Let me put it this way. Remember the last time your Jell-O mold came out in one piece? Did you ever make a layer cake that didn't stick to the pan? And, how did you feel the last time you went to unload the dishwasher and it was empty? Menu planning will make you feel like that every day!

If you haven't planned menus for a while, it may seem like a slow, methodical process at first, but stick with it and see if it's not everything I promised. Every time you do it you'll get faster and more efficient. Keep reading for how-to's.

THE CHOICE IS YOURS

The next time you're watching TV, riding as a passenger in the car, or taking a break at work, glance through one of your cookbooks. Using a color felt tip pen draw a circle around any recipes that seem tasty and those that will fit your time and money budgets.

Circle recipes that take less than ten minutes to prepare, not counting actual cooking time. Recipes with approximately five ingredients or less are usually the quickest and least time-consuming.

When scanning the list of ingredients notice if any are unusual or not easily available. You'll have better luck picking recipes that call for ingredients you normally have on hand. Also, does the dish require special tools, pans, or other equipment? If the meal will in any way complicate your life, forget it.

Go through a few of your favorite cookbooks and recipe files in this manner. And if you spot a recipe in a newspaper or magazine, don't rip it out until you've analyzed it in light of the criteria above. As much as possible, be sure it's a winner before it's selected.

When it comes time to actually plan your meals, you'll have a nice potpourri at your fingertips. Time pressure is often used as an excuse to avoid meal plans. This exercise will show you what a veritable gold mine of quick and easy recipes you have at your command.

As soon as you have a cache of recipes (both new ideas and old favorites), sit down once every week or two (or once a month) and come up with as many plans as you need. That way you can coordinate your recipes with coupons, sales, and in-season harvests. Plan ten to fifteen meals and have all the necessary ingredients on hand. Then when you discover exactly what the day is going to be like, you can pick out an appropriate menu, that takes into account your mood (a prime consideration), energy level, and schedule.

For years, when our children were younger, I used a two-month schedule. I got two monthly calendars, the type with large squares, and wrote down in each square the meal I would fix for dinner every night for the next two months. Of course, I left a few days each month blank so I could try a few recipes now and then or use up leftovers. I was careful to repeat the family favorites every two weeks or so. Because of schedule conflicts, mood swings, sickness, or other unpredictable events, it was occasionally necessary to switch Monday's planned meal with Tuesday's and so forth. But, basically I made up the schedule and never planned menus again for a whole year.

If you like the rotation idea you might want to try what my sister did. She set up seasonal menu plans, one for fall/winter and another for spring/summer.

Breakfast, Lunch, and Dinner

I don't formally plan menus for breakfast or lunch, but I do refer to a chart I found in my old home ec notes. Using this in unison with your knowledge of the basic four food groups will assure you and your family of a nutritious, well-planned diet.

For breakfast and lunch I simply refer to this chart and come up with spur-of-the-moment choices, though I'm careful to have plenty of breakfast and lunch staples on hand. Dinner plans are, however, physically written down and planned for, since dinner preparation time and clean-up is more extensive. The amount of time you spend planning is in direct proportion to the amount of time you save.

Time permitting, I do ahead as much of the meal as possible during breakfast and have one cleanup instead of two. Sometimes I tape instructions to the front of a cupboard door so the kids will know what to do when they get home.

TIME-SAVING CAPERS

In carpentry, when you join boards by interlocking wedge-shaped tenons and spaces, you are "dovetailing" or making a dovetailed

	Light	Medium	Hearty
Breakfast	Fruit or juice	Fruit or juice	Fruit or juice
	Cereal	Main dish	Cereal
	Bread	Bread	Main dish
	Beverage	Beverage	Bread or break- fast sandwich
			Beverage
Lunch	Soup	Soup	Salad
	Sandwich	Salad	Soup
	Beverage	Bread or sand- wich	Bread or sand- wich
		Beverage	Main dish
			Beverage
			Dessert, optional
Dinner	Main dish	Salad	Appetizer
	Vegetables	Main dish	Salad
	Bread	Vegetables	Main dish
	Beverage	Bread	Vegetables
	Dessert, optional	Beverage	Bread
		Dessert, optional	Beverage
			Dessert, optional

joint. If you interlock your knuckles you'll get the picture of what this joint looks like. We're going to do the same thing with menu planning by meshing today's meal preparation with tomorrow's.

Now that your recipes for the week's dinners are planned, look at the list and notice any similarities. Here are some examples. How many meals require chopped onions? Chop enough for the whole week and store the unused portion in an airtight container in the refrigerator. Are you planning meatloaf? It takes about six minutes to throw one together (including clean-up); it takes seven minutes to make three. With only a one-minute time investment you have two extra meals ready for the freezer. How many dishes during the month call for browned ground beef? Brown enough at one time to satisfy your month's needs and freeze in recipe-sized portions. This practice alone will save literally hours of time.

After shopping, begin preparing food for the coming week. Check the menus, shape hamburgers, cut up steak for stir-fry, wash vegetables, bake the chicken to be used for chicken salad, etc. This is a good time to get the kids involved.

Some people enjoy the convenience of having lunch box sandwiches ready during the week; after shopping is a perfect time to assemble sandwiches for the freezer. When packing lunches, just put the frozen sandwiches into the lunch box. When it's time to eat, the sandwiches are ready. But don't freeze mayonnaise or tomatoes, as the bread may become soggy.

Squeeze as much advance preparation from your shopping time as you can manage. My friend Sherrill comes home after shopping and cooks all the meals for a whole week. Then, after work, she pulls out one of the meals and heats it up.

Don't just think of dovetailing in terms of food; processes can be dovetailed as well. For example: What needs to be shredded, diced, or chopped this week? When you're shredding cheese for tonight's tacos you might as well shred the cabbage for tomorrow's cole slaw, and carrots for vegetable meatballs. As long as you have the food processor whirring, make the most of it and you'll only have to clean it once. When those future meals come up, you'll be glad you did.

What else can be done ahead of time? If Jell-O salad is planned for Tuesday night, note it on Monday's schedule in your calendar. Get it ready while cleaning up Monday's dinner. Also, after dinner is a good time to section grapefruit for breakfast or make orange juice. After any meal is a good time to make tomorrow's dessert, assemble sack lunches, make salad dressing, and so on.

Baking is another process that's easy to dovetail. Let's say you've prepared lasagne. Put it (or better yet, two) in the oven and prepare oven-steamed rice at the same time. A simple re-heating will have the rice table-ready for tomorrow's supper. Speaking of lasagne, I can make my quick recipe in fifteen minutes. (See page 127.) To double the recipe (giving me a backup meal for the freezer) takes seventeen minutes.

It just doesn't make sense to use maximum preparation times for every meal you prepare, when you can dovetail and make two main dishes in almost half the time. Now you can see what a costly mistake *no* planning is.

Here are some ways I dovetail our family meals. A large batch of meatloaf gives me the makings for: salisbury steaks, filled meat-roll, grape jelly meatballs, manicotti, meatball stroganoff, or many other main dishes. With extra mashed potatoes I can make potato puffs, hearty hamburger bake, and potato pancakes. Cooked potatoes are a necessary ingredient in potato salad, scrambled eggs and potatoes, hash browns, scalloped potatoes, and many more potato casseroles. Likewise, rice is simple to make in bulk. It keeps well and reheats easily. Extra cooked meat is especially good when served in a Chinese dish, stew, or soup.

Get into the habit of looking at the whole week's plan as you check tonight's scheduled fare. Continually ask questions like: Will I need potatoes (or whatever) again this week? Do I need to chop, shred, or dice something else? Can I use my blender or food processor for something else before I clean it and put it away?

One of the greatest aids to effective dovetailing is a plastic bag sealer. Leftover (or planned over) food is placed in a "boiling bag" and then it's sealed with the aid of a bag sealer. The food can be refrigerated or frozen. When it's time to reheat this food, just drop the bag into a pan of boiling water. The added advantage is there's no cleanup.

Bag sealers are widely available (usually under $20) at discount or variety stores everywhere. Their compact design makes them easy to store, or they can be mounted on a wall near an electrical outlet.

If you really take off with the dovetailing idea (and you should) you might find it helpful to keep an additional form that lists the prepared dishes in your freezer. This list will serve as a reminder of stored foods and may well come to your rescue when you're in a pinch and need a good meal fast. (To determine the shelf life of frozen foods, consult your cookbook.) Included in this chapter is a sample of the one we use.

MANAGING YOUR RECIPE COLLECTION

Recipes can certainly add to a kitchen clutter problem. Most of us rip out one delicious-sounding recipe after another thinking *this* is the one that will hurdle us to fame and probably get us a spot on *Good Morning America.*

We hoard those helpful little booklets endemic to every woman's magazine. There's the sweetened condensed milk booklet, Jell-O pudding file cards, instructions for Bisquick impossible pies, the complete chocolate lover's guide. The Chubby Gourmet whips up a masterpiece on TV and we feverishly scribble down a record of his every move. Luncheon dates with friends provide us with yet another source of recipes. Our friends share their latest find and we grab whatever's handy—check book deposit slips, napkins, shopping bags—and write down the details. We tear into food packages, ripping off the great recipes located on the back. We have stacks of once-irresistible cookbooks and file boxes crammed with our good intentions. We were going to try those recipes someday.

PREPARED DISHES IN FREEZER

Name of Dish	Date Prepared	Number Servings	Use by Date

Where do you put all this paper? How do you keep your kitchen from looking like the dead-file storage warehouse at American Express? There are a few logical solutions, none of which suggest tossing recipes into a drawer, shoving them in between cookbook covers, or wedging them into file boxes!

If you want to save recipes and still be able to find them in anything less than three hours, you need to round up a few simple supplies. Get a stack of file folders and give them the following headings (or make up your own): appetizers and dips, beverages, biscuits and bread, breakfast, cakes and frostings, casseroles, cookies, desserts and puddings, meat, fish, poultry, pies and pastries, salads and dressings, sandwiches, sauces, soups and stews, vegetables, miscellaneous. Stand them up in a plastic vegetable bin, dishpan, or cardboard box. Or use an expanding file. Now when you come across a new recipe you'll have a logical and efficient holding place for it.

Next, go through your recipe card file and toss out anything you don't want. Then, pull out every recipe you have never tried and file them according to category in the file folders.

Pick up a preprinted pack of recipe card dividers with headings similar to the ones you put on the file folders and file the remaining tried and true "keepers" behind the tabbed dividers in the card file. For a large collection, use a kitchen drawer.

Now that the box is organized, use it only for the family favorites—the standards you've always relied on. Don't clutter up the card file with recipes you've never tried or will likely never use, *even* if they're given to you on a recipe card.

If you're a booklet saver (and who isn't) you'll need an expanding file (with one large pocket) to house your collection. The file is sturdy enough to stand on a shelf next to the cookbooks and its open top design makes it easy to flip through your collection and choose just the booklet you're looking for.

Convert an extra drawer into a recipe card file.

Now, take a look at your cookbook collection and divide it into *A* and *C* stacks. The *A*'s and *B*'s stay in the kitchen, the *C*'s are out. Put them with your other books in another room. They'll still be available for occasional use or perusal but they won't be wasting potentially functional usage/storage kitchen space.

From this point on, whenever you get a new recipe idea take an extra two seconds and place it in the proper file folder. When you try the recipe and like it, copy it onto an index card (or affix the recipe itself to the card) and file it in the card file of tried and true favorites. If the recipe was undesirable for some reason, throw it out . . . now.

Here are two variations: Rather than keep your tried and trues in a card file, print the recipes on Rolodex cards and snap them into the Rolodex file. Flip to the needed recipe. The file stays open, keeping the recipe card visible. That way, you never have to take out and refile recipe cards.

Or try this: Put the recipes into magnetic photo albums. One TV anchor I know has an efficient system. She keeps vegetable and salad ideas in a green book; meat and main dishes go in the red book; desserts go in the yellow one; and so on.

Your card file can serve as a complete recipe index. If you can't remember which cookbook has your favorite recipe for Beef Stroganoff, let's say, make up a card for the file:

Beef Stroganoff
COMPANY'S COMING, page 43

Use the margins in your cookbooks and recipe cards to record the following: time it takes to prepare the dish and uses of the dish as a leftover. Also it helps to mark the ingredients located in the refrigerator with a yellow highlighter pen so you can gather them up in one trip and bring them to the mixing center.

To encourage yourself to try new recipes, here's an idea. Whenever you get a new recipe, post it on the refrigerator and give yourself one week (or so) to try it. When the designated time is up, if you still haven't tried it, throw it out.

A good way to perk up banal, boring meals is to periodically review those quick recipes you circled earlier. There's nothing like a few new ideas to rekindle your interest and motivation.

Menu Selection Sheets

Menu selection sheets are real time-savers, but because they're a little extra work they will probably only appeal to second-mile-goers. Menu selection sheets are lists of all the main dishes we eat for dinner. The dishes are listed by protein category: beef, ground beef, cheese and eggs, chicken, pork and ham, fish and seafood. I've also made listings for side dishes, particularly those featuring potatoes, rice, and dried beans.

Contained on the menu selection sheets are: the name of the dish, ingredients called for, reference (tells me where the recipe is located) and if the major portions of the dish can be used in another form as a leftover. I've included a sample form for you to photocopy. Start one sheet for each category: beef, chicken, fish, etc.

If you don't have time to fill out all the forms in one fell swoop, just add to it whenever you have a few extra minutes. One *Confessions of an Organized Housewife* reader wrote to say how much she enjoyed using her menu selection sheets. She filled out her forms while commuting back and forth to work and said it only took her about two weeks to complete the project.

Menu selection sheets have many benefits, the obvious being a tremendous meal planning assistance. When planning your meals, just flip through the sheets and all the choices are right there in front of you. No need to rely on memory or pore over a stack of books or index cards. Having the sheets handy in my planner allows me to plan meals wherever I am and I capitalize on odd moments—moments that would otherwise be wasted.

If I notice a sale on round steak advertised in the newspaper, I just flip to the menu selection sheets to see the different ways I use round steak and I'm also appraised of other ingredients I have to pick up in order to make those dishes. The ingredients list is a handy guide for using coupons and leftovers, too.

Now that you've seen the whole picture, here's the bare bones plan—the minimum meal-planning requirements:

1. Look for and mark quick and easy recipes.
2. Plan menus for at least ten days.
3. If possible, begin dinner after breakfast. (Thaw meat, soak beans, put a meal in the crock pot.)
4. Dovetail preparations and processes whenever possible.

MENU SELECTION SHEET

Name of Dish	Ingredients	Reference	Leftover

BON MOTS FOR THE BON VIVANT

- If you're a compulsive recipe clipper, designate one small dishpan or box to hold collected recipe finds. When the container is full, don't save any more recipes until you've filed your collection. That'll keep the clutter within manageable limits.

- If a recipe calls for an unusual ingredient, mark in with a blue highlighter pen (or any color other than your "refrigerated item" one). Then, even without reading the entire recipe, you'll be reminded to buy the ingredient.

- Post a copy of the week's dinner menus. In the morning you'll be instantly reminded of what to take out of the freezer and what dovetailing preparations to begin. Also, diet-conscious folks can plan their "away from home" food accordingly. (Most fast food chains will furnish you with a nutrition and calorie guide on request.)

- Save weekly menus, grocery lists and dated cash register tape. Staple them together and file for a quick reference for future meals and their approximate cost.

- If you want to prepare a time-consuming dish but don't have enough time, see if you can break down the recipe into two work sessions (pre-measure ingredients and mix later, for example).

- Assemble all needed ingredients and utensils before you start meal preparations. How many times, for example, have you been rolling dough and had to reach (with floured hands) into the drawer to get the biscuit cutter?

- Clear, plastic report covers keep cookbook pages clean. Open the book, place the center crease of the report cover down the center of the book. Any splashes can be wiped off.

- For recipe cards, stand a fork (tines up) in a tall glass and place the card in the tines. Or use a magnet on the refrigerator or oven hood. If you use a metal recipe file, the magnet can be stored on the lid.

- Razor-sharp knives save time. Check in the Yellow Pages for someone near you who can get your knives back into shape. Thereafter, keep them sharp with one of the many knife sharpeners currently on the market.

- Use only one set of measuring cups by measuring dry ingredients first, then wet.

- Rinse off utensils (knives, spoons, measuring equipment, etc.) when cooking or baking and use them again instead of reaching for clean duplicates.

- Frying food in a Dutch oven is less messy than a conventional frying pan. Because of its high sides, it keeps the grease from splattering.

- To cook several small dishes at once in the electric frying pan, mold small cups out of aluminum foil and place in the pan.

- A bundt or tube baking pan can be used for many things besides cakes. It holds stuffed peppers or potatoes, too. To cut corn off the cob, stand the corn on the tube and cut off the kernels; they fall neatly into the pan below. Bake meatloaf in a tube pan or set a gelatin salad. After unmolding, serve meatloaf sauce or whipped topping in the center hole.

- To easily remove baked potatoes from the oven, bake them in muffin tins.

- Spring action food scoops (ice-cream scoops) come in all sizes and are good measuring cups for shortening and peanut butter. (Dip the scoop in water to keep food from sticking.) They're also handy when making meatballs and drop cookies. To fill baking cups for muffins or cupcakes—use a scoop! When buying a scoop, sometimes the size (i.e., ⅛ cup, ½ cup, etc.) is printed right on the package. If not, it's easy to determine the scoop's volume. Fill it with water and pour the water into a clear measuring cup to see how much the scoop holds. The ⅛ cup (perfect for cookies, meatballs, cupcakes, and muffins) and the ⅓ cup (good for ice cream and dishing food servings) are the two common denominators for any recipe, so they're the most useful sizes.

- Before forming meatballs or Rice Krispie treats, slightly dampen your hands. (If you're using a meatballer, dampen it frequently during use.) This keeps the food from sticking to you or the instrument you're working with.
- Mix meatloaf with your potato masher.
- As a filling for stuffed green peppers, mash leftover meatloaf and moisten it with a small amount of tomato juice. Stuff peppers and bake. Top with grated cheese in the last five minutes of baking.
- Scrub vegetables well and cook without paring them.
- Use a French fryer basket when boiling potatoes, pasta, or hard boiled eggs. It's safer and easier than draining the hot water from the pan.
- When peeling boiled potatoes, rub a little shortening on your hands and the knife blade. This will keep the peelings from clinging to you.
- Instead of discarding potato water, add it (along with some powdered milk) to the mashed potatoes instead of refrigerated milk. Also, the potato water can be used when making gravy.
- Always cook enough potatoes or rice for more than one meal.
- Cook bacon and flash freeze. Heat separate pieces as needed.
- Drain bacon, sausage, fish, or other fried foods on styrofoam meat trays or in the top of an egg carton. (Line with paper towels.)
- Styrofoam meat trays have many uses, and they're available

in any butcher department for a few cents each. They're good for slicing onions (and keep the strong odor off the cutting board) and tomatoes. They're good for carting cookies, brownies, or other such goodies and you won't have to worry about losing your dish. Use them for freezing snack bars and cookies and for mailing cookies and candy. Broken up in small pieces, styrofoam trays provide good drainage in flower pots.

- Recycled plastic lids are good saucers for drippy bottles. They can also be used as coasters.

- Combine salt and pepper into one shaker. A good combination is ³⁄₄ C salt and ¹⁄₄ C pepper.

- For "instant" white sauce mix 1 cup softened butter with 1 cup flour. Spread in ice cube tray (or other shallow container) and chill. Cut into eight equal-sized cubes. Freeze. To make white sauce (medium thick) put one cube into 2 cups of cold milk. Heat, stirring until sauce is thickened. Add salt and pepper, if desired.

- The pointed end of a beverage can opener is good for deveining shrimp, hulling strawberries, or ripping into boxes.

- A small crochet hook is a good tool for deveining shrimp.

- A dough cutter is handy for cutting sandwiches.

- Make miniature hamburger buns for children by cutting crusts of bread with a biscuit cutter.

- Instead of chopping eggs for egg salad, try grating them, or use a pastry blender to finely chop.

- Spray kitchen shears with cooking spray before cutting dates and figs. (Or dip the scissors in water.)

- Use your potato masher when making juice from frozen concentrates. You'll find the concentrate melts much more quickly.

- Make Jell-O fast in a 1-quart measure. Add I cup boiling water to the Jell-O and stir to dissolve. Note the liquid level and add ice to increase it by 1 cup. Stir until ice is melted. Set in the refrigerator until firm or thick enough to hold fruit, etc.

- Save leftover lemon, orange, and lime rinds and freeze. The rinds grate easily when frozen.

- If bananas are too ripe and you haven't time to make banana bread or cookies, the banana pulp can be frozen and used up when you do have time.

- To make cinnamon toast, combine sugar and cinnamon (according to taste) and keep in an empty salt shaker. Or, if you prefer, mix the sugar and cinnamon and blend into soft margarine or butter. Store in the refrigerator. That way you eliminate the mess of sprinkling.

- A paper towel under the bottom piece of toast on the plate keeps it from getting soggy.

- Melt chocolate in boiling bags. These bags are also good for marinating meat. (Boiling bags can be purchased in large supermarkets and wherever bag sealers are sold.)

- Measure dry ingredients for cookies, cakes, etc., onto a sheet of waxed paper or paper towel. That way you can make the dessert using only one bowl. When making a cake, scrape the bowl clean and make the frosting right in the same bowl.

- Whenever you're making cake, cookies, brownies, etc., measure extra dry ingredients, label and store for a quick assembly next time.

- Keep a shaker container filled with flour in the mixing center. It's good for dusting baking pans or food that is to be floured before cooking.

- When making something that requires the addition of beaten egg whites (waffles, for example) beat the egg whites first, then beat the batter. That way you won't need to clean the beaters first.

- To retrieve a piece of egg shell that has dropped into the food, use a large clean piece of the shell. (This is the best idea I've come across in years! It really works.)

- Slightly dampen the countertop with water and spread a piece of plastic wrap smoothly over the dampened area. Flour the plastic and roll out dough.

- Roll out biscuits and cut into squares. This saves you from re-rolling the cut-up dough over and over.

- When making refrigerator cookies, press the dough into large frozen juice cans and chill. When ready to bake, open the bottom of the can and push the dough out for slicing, using the can's edge as a cutting guide.

- Store batches of cookie dough in margarine tubs in the freezer. Bake as needed for hot, freshly made cookies.

- Freeze broken cookies and when you've got a supply, crush them and use in crumb cookie crust.

- An ice bucket makes a great cookie jar.

- Put a marshmallow in the bottom of an ice cream cone to keep it from leaking.

- When serving Sloppy Joes to children, scoop out some of the hamburger bun. That way the sandwich filling will be "in" the bun instead of "on" it.

- An ironing board set at the proper height is a good temporary table for children.

- Washcloths and hand towels are good napkins and placemats. A washcloth is also a good napkin for a lunch box meal.

- Use a loud dinner bell (or cow bell) to call the kids in for dinner.

- When teaching kids to cook, start by making snacks and breakfast.

- For busy families, try having alternate mealtimes or meal styles. Have dinner after school and snacks before bed. Or, if everyone is eating a hearty lunch away from home, have a typical lunch-type meal at dinner time.

chapter 7

SHOPPING SAVVY

If your name is Indiana Jones; if you can bench press a good-sized farm animal; if you're as good with numbers as Jimmy the Greek, E. F. Hutton, or Johnny Carson's CPA, then you've got all the skills you need to become a super-shopper.

It's a jungle out there. Inexperienced cartpushers, kids pleading for treats (and sometimes for mercy), shopping carts that always bear to the left, sales to spot, fruit to pinch, toilet paper to squeeze. Finding the Ark of the Covenant was easier than trying to locate the Butter Buds, water chestnuts, and kumquats in anything less than two hours.

Even so, I'm here to offer a ray of hope. If you're always standing in the slowest line, grabbing unpriced goods off the shelves, and causing major traffic jams at the check-out while the stock boy goes to verify the price, you (yes, you) can still acquire the spirit of adventure, the stamina, and the fiscal prowess you need to survive the cartpushers' game. Here are the rules of play.

TO MARKET, TO MARKET WITH A LIST

Ralph Nader would be proud. I, too, will follow the other consumer advocates and recommend (make that insist) that you shop from an organized list. How many times have you heard that suggestion? Sure, you've heard it over and over; but making a list takes time and that's one thing you haven't got. So you skip the planning step, walk unprepared through the supermarket, and join the ranks of countless supermarket casualties. Seeming victims of amnesia, they walk down each aisle glancing left and right like the spectators at Wimbledon, hoping the flashy displays and snappy pictures will remind them of things they need to buy.

Approximately 60 percent of shoppers do not use a list, and thus they play into the market's hands. Without a list you spend extra time in the store piling up one impulse purchase after another almost in sync with the whir of the cash register. The longer you spend in the market's confines, the more time and money you waste.

Every trip to the store is more time-costly than you may think. Even "just running in for a few things" involves parking the car, searching the shelves, sampling demonstrated products, standing in line, traveling time to and from the store, and finding the car in the parking lot.

The decisions you make in the grocery aisle usually bear little, if any, relation to your actual grocery needs. A carefully planned list puts an end to this gross waste of time. It prevents you from forgetting an important item so you won't have to squander even more time on repeat performances. An organized list, with like products grouped together, allows you to select needed items without having to backtrack through the aisles, fighting traffic and temptation. If I remember correctly, it's a principle of plane geometry: the shortest distance between two points is a straight line. In the grocery store the shortest distance between the entrance and the exit is a route guided by such a carefully planned list.

Hang a spiral tablet or small clipboard on the inside of your mixing center cupboard door and bolt (need I say why?) a pen or pencil to it. This will serve as a perpetual grocery list for the whole family to contribute to. Tell them what it's for and ask them to jot down anything they use up or notice is in short supply.

Before your next shopping trip add to this list the ingredients needed for the week's planned menus. Then rip off the page, or take the whole clipboard to the store.

Aside from making you look like the patron saint of the supermarket, the clipboard is quite handy. The clip holds coupons you're planning to use, bottle deposit receipts, or trading stamps. It stands in the child's seat in the cart and is always in full view, making it easy to check things off as you pull them from the shelves. This is much better than juggling a list in your hand that will inevitably be ripped, mangled, and chewed on before you even get to the gum-ball machines.

Some people like to write their lists on envelopes and slip coupons and notes for other errands inside. If this is your wont, just clip a stack of envelopes to the clipboard and hang it in the mixing center. When you leave the store, the envelope fits easily into your pocket or purse.

Or, perhaps you'll like this idea: make up a bunch of pre-printed shopping lists. Divide a sheet of paper into ten general headings: breads and cereals, canned, convenience foods, dairy, frozen, health and beauty aids, household and miscellaneous, meat, produce, staples and condiments. Another option is to divide the paper into four main food groups and add a nonfood miscellane-ous column.

With a generalized list like this you can go into any store and shop like an old customer without chasing back and forth gather-ing up products. Also, if you have enlisted help, you can tear off sections and have everyone in charge of a separate group. If other people are helping you shop, be sure that sizes of cans and pack-ages, quantities, preferred brands or grades, and acceptable substi-tutes are spelled out clearly on the list.

Being a touch absent-minded myself (and that's an under-statement), I go one step further. Somehow, my addled brain is able to remember my planning notebook, so I always have it with me wherever I go. But trying to remember two things (the notebook and a shopping list) seemed to overload the circuit and the list was usually left at home lying on the kitchen table. So I decided to keep the list inside my planner and it's proven to be a very successful idea. Now, I never forget the list and even when I'm driving around town and decide to go shopping at the spur of the moment, I'm effi-ciently prepared.

I shop once a week, usually on Friday, so I put a paper clip (to serve as a bookmark) on the upcoming Friday's daily calendar page. Then I insert a blank shopping list form (see illustration). Every time I need to add an item to the list, I flip open the calendar to Fri-day (using the paperclip as a guide) and jot it down in the appropri-ate category.

While I'm working around the house I make a record of things I notice are running low: paper towels, toothpaste, laundry deter-gent, notebook paper, silver polish, etc. I transfer the family's list on the clipboard to my planning notebook. And, on a weekly basis, I check inventory sheets and menu plans, adding products as nec-essary.

Breads and Cereals

_____

_____

_____

_____

Canned Goods

_____

_____

_____

Convenience Foods

_____

_____

_____

Dairy Products and Eggs

_____

_____

_____

Frozen Foods

_____

_____

_____

Health and Beauty Aids

_____

_____

_____

_____

Household and Miscellaneous

_____

_____

_____

Meat

_____

_____

_____

Produce

_____

_____

_____

Staples and Condiments

_____

_____

_____

This sounds like a major undertaking, but I want to stress that this only takes a few minutes—as does any list. Remember, this three-minute investment could save you hours because you won't have to run back to the store for forgotten and desperately needed items.

The most important thing is to *always shop from an organized list*. If you pursue that objective alone and ignore what I'm about to recommend, that's okay. Nevertheless, there are two more steps you can take which will help you maximize your shopping efficiency and minimize the amount of time you spend in the store.

These suggestions do require a slight time investment, so I'm afraid three-quarters of you will likely read through the following advice and consider it good material for a remake of the *Twilight Zone*. Although I must admit to having a penchant for this kind of stuff, I have found these methods enormously successful.

Fasten your seat belts. Here we go.

YOU MAY NEVER RUN OUT OF BREAD AGAIN

Once upon a time I dreamed about the hours I would save if we never ran out of bread, dishwasher detergent, or potatoes. Considering the prospect motivated me to action, so I sat down and made a rough list of everything I ever bought at the supermarket. When I went grocery shopping, my memory was aided by the array of products displayed on the shelves. I quickly noted every item I had forgotten to include on the original list, and within a few weeks the list was complete. With the aid of my brother's Apple II, I alphabetized the list and arranged another by category.

Scanning the categorized list, I ticked off each item I wanted to keep in stock. These were the things I never wanted to run out of again. I was very selective, but I determined that these items would be bonafide *A*'s. Next, I typed up a categorized mini list that contained only those high-priority *A* items and put the chart in my planning notebook.

Here's how the system works. I always keep at least one of each *A* in stock and one in use. For example, I never want to run out of toothpaste again, so I keep one tube in use and one in the supply cupboard. When the one in use is gone, I get the reserve tube and add "toothpaste" to the weekly shopping list. If you have ample storage space, then you can have more than one backup stored. However, to keep your stockpile supplied, be sure to add each depleted product to the shopping list as soon as it's used up.

The *A* priority list has come to the rescue many times. Occasionally I go through the list, checking it against the supplies on the shelves, just to make sure we've got at least one of each product in reserve. Whenever you're short of funds, you'll automatically know where to spend the money you *do* have—on those *A*'s. And if you're occasionally impulsive and stop off at a store unprepared, flip to your *A* priority list and use it as a guide. Even this insouciant approach is better than relying on memory alone.

Next, I dealt with the alphabetized list. We usually shop at *one* of three supermarkets, so I went through each store, clipboard in hand, and wrote down roughly how the store was organized. (Basically, I just copied down the overhead hanging signs that tell you what's in each aisle.) Then using the alphabetized list, I transferred the information to the store guide form.

Now, I know when I'm at Joe's Market, for example, that the sweet pickles are in aisle 3A, the bread in 4B, and the mascara in

IGA	Kroger	Joe's Market	STORE GUIDE
15	6A	SWW	Air Freshener
12	14B	6	Aluminum Foil
13	15A	7	Ammonia
3	2B	4	Applesauce
9	8A	SWW	Aspirin
16	13A	1	Baby Food
NWW	SEW	WW	Bacon

15A. This, then, has become my master list and I keep it (you guessed it) in my planning notebook. I have never spent a minute looking for anything since I drew up this chart and it's perfect for directing the kids. Sometimes I'll stay in the car and send one of the kids into the store for something. Telling them exactly where each item is located certainly speeds up the process. Some products are not necessarily located in an aisle. In those cases I refer to the northwest wall (NWW), southeast entrance (SEE), etc.

With an alphabetized list and blank store form included in the book, I've really done most of the work for you. All you need to do is: Photocopy a few store guide forms, fill in your list of selected grocery products (using the alphabetized list as a reminder), then add the store's layout. In this illustration, by the way, you'll notice I've listed the products according to how our family refers to them. for example, Kleenex is really facial tissue, but we always call it Kleenex (no matter what brand it is). So that's how it's written.

Either the alphabetized or categorized master list can be pared down to suit your needs, duplicated, and hung up in the mixing center to serve as your grocery list. (If your list won't fit on one page, have it reduced at a quick copy outlet.) Just check off the items you need to purchase.

I'm not advocating that you get carried away with organizing your list; too much organizing is as wasteful as none. The purpose of a careful inventory is to help you get everything you need in as few trips as possible and to help you go quickly. If you can do that, no further organization is necessary.

Store Guide Form

MASTER GROCERY LIST

Air freshener
Aluminum foil
Ammonia
Applesauce
Aspirin
Baby food
Baby formula
Bacon
Baked beans
Bakery (fresh)
Baking chocolate
Baking powder
Baking soda
Barbecue sauce
Bar soap
Bathroom tissue
Beans
Beans, dried
Bean sprouts
Beef, dried
Beets
Biscuit mix
Bisquick
Bleach
Blueberries, canned
Bouillon cubes
Bread
Bread crumbs
Bread dough, frozen
Broccoli, frozen
Brooms

Brown sugar
Buns
Burritos
Butter
Butter Buds
Buttermilk
Buttermilk, powdered
Cake decorations
Cake mixes
Candy
Canned biscuits
Canned fruit
Canned vegetables
Carpet Fresh
Cereal, boxed
Charcoal and lighter fluid
Cheese
Cheese spreads
Cheetos
Cheez Whiz
Chicken, canned
Chili
Chili beans
Chili sauce
Chinese food
Chocolate, baking
Chocolate chips
Chop suey vegetables
Chow mein noodles
Clams, canned
Clams, fresh

Cleaners

Cleanser

Cocoa

Cocoa mix

Coconut

Cookie mixes

Cookies

Cooking spray

Cooking utensils

Cool-Whip

Corn

Corn bread mix

Cornmeal

Corn starch

Corn syrup

Cosmetics

Cottage cheese

Crab, canned

Crab, fresh

Cream

Cream cheese

Creamed corn

Cream of Wheat

Croutons

Cupcake cups

Dairy products

Deodorant

Desserts, frozen

Dietetic foods

Dinners, frozen

Dips

Dishwasher detergent

Dishwashing liquid

Disposable diapers

Distilled water

Dried beef

Dried fruit

Drink mixes

Eggs

Enchilada sauce

Enfamil

English muffins

Evaporated milk

Fabric softener

Feminine hygiene

First Aid

Fish, fresh

Fish, frozen

Flour

Foil

Freezer wrap

French fries

Fried rice

Fritos

Fruit, canned

Fruit cocktail

Fruit, dried

Fruit, fresh

Fruit, frozen

Fruit rolls

Gelatin

Gourmet foods

Graham crackers

Granola bars

Gravy, canned

Gravy, mixes

Green chilies
Hair care products
Hair spray
Ham
Hardware
Honey
Hot dogs
Ice cream
Ice-cream cones
Ice-cream toppings
Insecticides
Jam
Jell-O
Jelly
Juice, baby
Juices, bottled
Juices, canned
Juices, frozen
Karo syrup
Ketchup
Kidney beans
Kitty litter
Kleenex
Kool-Aid
Laundry detergent
Lemon juice
Lentils
Light bulbs
Liquid hand soap
Lotions
Lunch bags
Luncheon meat
Macaroni and cheese

Malt-O-Meal
Mandarin oranges
Maraschino cherries
Margarine
Marinade mix
Marshmallows
Matches
Mayonnaise
Meat
Meat, canned
Melon balls
Mexican food
Milk
Milk, powdered
Mixed vegetables
Mops
Mouthwash
Mushrooms
Mustard
Napkins
Noodles
Nuts
Oatmeal
Olive oil
Olives
Onion rings, canned
Onion rings, frozen
Oysters, canned
Oysters, fresh
Pancake mix
Pantyhose
Paper cups
Paper plates

Paper towels
Parmesan cheese
Pasta
Peaches, canned
Peanut butter
Peanuts
Pears, canned
Peas, canned
Peas, dried
Pepper
Pet food
Pharmacy
Picante sauce
Pickles
Pie crusts
Pie filling, canned
Pimentos
Pineapple, canned
Pizza, frozen
Pizza mix
Pizza Quick
Plastic bags
Plastic scrubber
Plasticware
Plastic wrap
Plums, canned
Popcorn
Popsicles
Pork and beans
Potato chips
Pot pies
Poultry
Powdered buttermilk

Powdered milk
Powdered sugar
Preserves
Pretzels
Prewash spray
Produce
Pudding, canned
Pudding, mix
Pumpkin, canned
Q-Tips
Raisins
Raspberries, frozen
Razors
Refried beans
Relish
Rice
Rice-A-Roni
Ritz crackers
Romano cheese
Salad dressing mixes
Salad dressings
Salmon, canned
Salmon, fresh
Salsa
Salt
Saltines
Sanitary napkins
Sauce mixes
Sauerkraut
Sausage
Sausage, canned
Seafood, fresh
Seasoning mixes

Shampoo
Shaving aids
Shortening
Shrimp, canned
Shrimp, fresh
Shrimp, frozen
Soda crackers
Soft drinks
SOS
Soup, canned
Soup, dry
Sour cream
Soy sauce
Spam
Spices
Starch, laundry
Stews, canned
Straws
Stuffing mix
Sugar
Sunflower seeds
Sweet potatoes, canned
Sweet-sour sauce
Tobasco sauce
Taco sauce
Taco shells, boxed
Taco shells, fresh
Tampons
Tartar sauce
Tater tots
Teriyaki sauce
Toilet bowl cleaner
Toilet paper

Tomato paste
Tomato sauce
Tomatoes, canned
Toothpaste
Tortillas, boxed
Tortilla chips
Tortillas, fresh
Trash can liners
Tuna
TV dinners
Vanilla
Vegetable oil
Vegetables, canned
Vegetables, fresh
Vegetables, frozen
Vinegar
Waffles, frozen
Water chestnuts
Wax paper
Wet wipes
Wheat germ
Wheat Hearts
Wheat Thins
Whipped topping, boxed
Whipping cream
Windex
Worcestershire sauce
Yams
Yeast
Yogurt
Ziploc bags

CATEGORIZED MASTERLIST

BREADS AND CEREALS

Bakery, fresh
Bread
Bread crumbs
Buns
Cereal
Cream of Wheat
Croutons
English muffins
Malt-O-Meal

Oatmeal
Tortillas, fresh
Wheat Hearts

_____

_____

_____

_____

_____

CANNED GOODS

Applesauce
Baby Food
Baby Formula
Baked beans
Beans
Bean sprouts
Beets
Blueberries
Bouillon cubes
Chicken
Chili
Chili beans
Chinese food
Chow Mein noodles
Clams
Corn

Crab
Creamed corn
Dried beef
Enchilada sauce
Evaporated milk
Fruit, canned
Fruit cocktail
Gourmet Foods
Gravy
Green chilies
Juice
Kidney beans
Mandarin oranges
Meat
Mexican food
Mixed vegetables

Mushrooms

Onion rings

Oysters

Peaches

Pears

Peas

Pet food

Picante sauce

Pimentos

Pineapple

Plums

Pork and beans

Pumpkin

Refried beans

Salmon

Salsa

Sauerkraut

Sausage, canned

Shrimp

Soup

Spam

Stews

Sweet potatoes

Sweet-sour sauce

Taco sauce

Teriyaki sauce

Tomato paste

Tomatoes

Tuna

Vegetables

Water chestnuts

Yams

_____

_____

_____

_____

_____

CONVENIENCE AND SNACK FOODS

Cake decorations

Cake mixes

Candy

Cocoa mix

Cookie mix

Cookies

Corn bread mix

Cupcake cups

Dried fruit

Fritos

Fruit rolls

Graham crackers

Granola bars

Ice-cream cones

Ice-cream topping

Kool-Aid

Macaroni and cheese

Marshmallows

Nuts

Peanuts

Pizza mix
Pizza Quick
Popcorn
Potato chips
Pretzels
Pudding, canned
Pudding mix
Raisins
Rice-A-Roni
Ritz crackers
Salad dressing mixes
Saltines
Sauce mixes
Seasoning mixes

Soda crackers
Soft drinks
Stuffing mix
Sunflower seeds
Tortillas, boxed
Tortilla chips
Wheat Thins
Whipped topping, boxed

_____
_____
_____
_____
_____

DAIRY AND EGGS

Biscuits, canned
Butter
Butter Buds
Buttermilk
Cheese
Cheese spreads
Cheez Whiz
Cottage Cheese
Cream
Cream cheese
Dips
Eggs

Milk
Parmesan cheese
Pudding
Romano cheese
Whipping cream
Yogurt

_____
_____
_____
_____
_____

FROZEN

Bread dough
Broccoli

Burritos
Cool-Whip

Dinners
Fish
French fries
Fruit
Ice cream
Juice
Melon balls
Onion rings
Pie crusts
Pizza
Popsicles
Pot pies

Raspberries
Shrimp
Strawberries
TV dinners
Vegetables
Waffles
Whipped topping
_____
_____
_____
_____
_____

HEALTH AND BEAUTY AIDS

Aspirin
Bar soap
Bathroom tissue
Cosmetics
Deodorant
Feminine hygiene
First Aid
Hair care products
Hair spray
Kleenex
Liquid hand soap
Lotions
Mouthwash
Pantyhose

Pharmacy
Razors
Sanitary napkins
Shampoo
Shaving Aids
Tampons
Toilet paper
Toothpaste
_____
_____
_____
_____
_____

HOUSEHOLD AND MISCELLANEOUS

Air freshener
Aluminum foil
Ammonia
Bleach
Brooms
Carpet Fresh
Charcoal and lighter fluid
Chore Girl Scrubber
Cleaners
Cleanser
Cooking utensils
Dietetic foods
Dishwasher detergent
Dishwashing liquid
Disposable diapers
Distilled water
Fabric softener
Foil
Freezer wrap
Hardware
Insecticides
Kitty litter
Laundry detergent
Light bulbs
Lunch bags

Matches
Mops
Napkins
Paper cups
Paper plates
Paper towels
Plastic bags
Plastic scrubber
Plasticware
Plastic wrap
SOS
Prewash Spray
Starch
Straws
Toilet bowl cleaner
Trash can liners
Wet wipes
Windex
Ziploc bags

_____
_____
_____
_____
_____

MEAT, FISH, POULTRY

Bacon
Beef

Chicken
Clams

Crab   Shrimp
Fish   Turkey
Ham   _____
Hot dogs   _____
Luncheon meat   _____
Salmon   _____
Sausage   _____
Seafood

PRODUCE

Fresh fruits and vegetables

STAPLES AND CONDIMENTS

Baking chocolate   Flour
Baking powder   Gelatin
Baking soda   Honey
Barbecue sauce   Jam
Biscuit mix   Jelly
Bisquick   Karo syrup
Brown sugar   Ketchup
Buttermilk powder   Lemon juice
Chocolate, baking   Maraschino cherries
Chocolate chips   Marinade
Cocoa   Mayonnaise
Coconut   Mustard
Cooking spray   Noodles
Cornmeal   Olive oil
Corn starch   Olives
Corn syrup   Pancake mix

Pasta

Peanut butter

Pepper

Pickles

Pimentos

Powdered buttermilk

Powdered milk

Powdered sugar

Preserves

Relish

Rice

Salad dressings

Salt

Shortening

Spices

Sugar

Tobasco sauce

Tartar sauce

Vanilla

Vegetable oil

Vinegar

Wheat germ

Worcestershire sauce

Yeast

_____

_____

_____

_____

TO COUPON OR NOT TO COUPON

There has been a resurgence of interest in the cash-off coupon. So much so that few home managers can knowingly toss one out without suffering pangs of guilt, sweaty palms, or muscle spasms. In order to silence the harping, we usually rationalize by whispering, "I just don't have time to mess with coupons."

Effective use of coupons does, indeed, take time. The experts claim that you can save an average of 30 percent on your total grocery bill just by using coupons and refund offers. To realize this savings, however, you must file and trade coupons and refund offers; save refund qualifiers (boxes, labels, or virtually any other part of the product packaging); subscribe to at least one refunding newsletter; and carefully organize and execute shopping trips. To do this right takes approximately five hours a week.

That is a big time investment, but many refunders enjoy it as an exciting hobby—one that offers money in the mailbox almost every day. Still others treat couponing and refunding as an at-home part-time job. A few coupon queens have worked so hard and profited so well they now have it as a full-time job.

If you're interested in pursuing this savings plan seriously, I would recommend you read Susan Samtur's *Cashing In at the Check-out*. It's a short paperback that spells out all the fine points of couponing and refunding and lists several refunding newsletters you can subscribe to.

If, like most of us, you don't want to invest five hours a week, you can still take advantage of coupons without giving up any free time. Though the coupons do save some money I don't claim a 30 percent reduction with my system.

First of all, I purchased an expanding check file (made of tagboard) and labeled each pocket with various categories: beverages, cereals, condiments and staples, dairy, health and beauty aids, household, laundry, meat, miscellaneous, prepared (bottled, boxed, canned), snacks, fast food. I keep this file (closed with the self-closing elastic band) under the front seat of the car.

Next, I save only *big* coupons (25¢ or more) and I never rip out a coupon for something I wouldn't normally buy. Then, I shove the coupons into an envelope I carry in my purse. Whenever I'm waiting for someone while sitting in the car or whenever I'm a passenger in the car, I take out the envelope and the coupon file and put the coupons in their respective pockets. (If I'm driving, one of the kids does the filing.) About two to three times a year I use waiting time to look through the file and pull out expired coupons.

The beauty of the system is that I (whose body often takes off before my brain) never forget the coupons because they're always in the car. I can't begin to tell you how many times we've arrived at a store or a fast-food restaurant and wished we had the coupons with us. Now we store them at the point of first use—in the car!

If you want to take advantage of occasional refund offers that you come across, make an index card for each category in your coupon file and stick it in the pocket. Here's how the system works. Let's say there's a $1 refund if you buy three packages of Goodie Cookies and send in the proofs of purchase (POP's). Pull out the snack card and write: Goodie Cookies 3 POP's $1 refund. Then, stick the card back in the pocket. (For a casual couponer/refunder you can also file the refund form in the pocket with the coupons.) Now, let's say you're making Caramel Crumballs for dessert this week and you need to buy some cookies. Pull out the snack card and see if there's a refund on cookies. You'll be reminded of the Goodie Cookie offer and purchase that particular brand.

More serious money savers read grocery ads and plan their menus around store specials. They try to match up these sales with cash-off coupons and look for stores that "double coupon." They give you double the face value of a coupon. A 25¢ off coupon would be worth 50¢ off in a store whose policy is double couponing.

There are seldom cash-off coupons or refunds available for store brand merchandise. So, before you buy, see if you have a coupon for a name brand. With a coupon, a name brand may actually be cheaper than a house brand.

YOUR FOOD DOLLAR

In a 1985 Consumer Trends report, Louis Harris and Associates observed that saving money appears to be "out" and saving time "in." According to the publication, many shoppers are willing to spend money if it means they can save time.

If you're a part of that vanishing breed of consumer who still cares about how her food dollar is spent, here are some tried and true value-minded ideas.

- Always shop from a list and stick to the list. Don't be suckered into buying whatever the demonstrator is frying. She gets paid by the hour whether you buy the product or not, so don't feel obligated. The grocer is cashing in on the idea that if people are hungry (or tempted with food) they'll buy more. So follow the oft-repeated code: don't shop when you're hungry.

- Plan your shopping to last for at least a week. The less often you shop, the less you'll spend. Having your bread and milk delivered will keep you out of the store and thus save you money, even though the delivery service is slightly more expensive.

  If time is more scarce than money, find a market that will take your order by phone and deliver the products to you (or at least have them ready for you to pick up).

BUY THE WEIGH

- Unless the kids are trained not to grovel and beg, leave them home. They'll slow you down with their TV-brainwashed minds and wreak havoc with your budget. However, if you work out a deal such as "Everyone gets to pick out one nutritious thing he'd like to have this week," it can work to your advantage, especially if they'll help round up needed commodities from the far reaches of the store.

When shopping with very young children, take a man-sized belt to the store with you. (Stretch belts are good, too.) This belt makes a great shopping cart seat belt for the child. (Good for restaurants, too.)

- Avoid shopping during peak periods (from 5 to 6:30 p.m.) and on weekends. These early evening hours are the times when the folks who've been wondering all day what to fix for dinner do their shopping. They are a highly disorganized lot, so steer clear of them.

- Avoid buying food any place but a grocery store. Avoid excessive trips to restaurants and fast-food chains. The food is often twice as expensive as food you prepare yourself and is usually high in fat, sodium, and calories, and notoriously deficient in vitamins, minerals, and dietary fiber. You also pay more for food purchased from small stores or convenience shops. You get the most for your money when you shop at a large grocery store in a middle-class neighborhood.

  Avoid buying certain nonfood items in a grocery store (toys, plants, hardware, and so on). These are generally poorer quality and more expensive.

- Don't pay for a flashy store layout. There is one particular market in our town where I love to shop. It's so gorgeous! It's clean and well-stocked. You really feel great when you walk through the automatic electronic-eye doors. They even provide play shopping carts for little kids to push around. But the catch is the prices. The cost of anything in that store is so outrageous they might as well hold a gun to your head and say, "This is a stick up!" The price stickers sneer at you as if to say, "That'll be $2.79, sucker."

  Then there's another store that one of our kids feared was a dungeon and he wouldn't set foot in it until he was seven and one-half years old. The building is timeworn, the aisles are narrow, there are no bright lights or colorful banners. But, the produce is fresh, the checkers are fast and friendly, and it's the best value in town. Because the square footage of the store is somewhat limited, you can get in and out quickly without having to walk past motor oil, greeting cards, and furnace filters on your way to the bananas.

• Try to do all your shopping in one store. Plan your menus around that store's specials and don't chase around town picking up good deals from every merchant. This is almost always a costly mistake unless you are scrupulously well-disciplined, and the stores are close together. Stock up on your favorite products whenever your store is offering a special price. Shopping the same store has other advantages as well: you become familiar with the store layout and can shop faster; you get acquainted with the personnel and know which checkers are quick and dependable. It's also to your advantage to know the butcher and the produce and bakery managers, should you have unique requests or needs.

• Be aware of regular prices so you'll be able to recognize bona-fide sales and price reductions.

• Whatever is done to food before you buy it (slicing, cooking, premeasuring, prepackaging, flavoring, etc.) costs you money. Unless the product proves to be a great time-saving convenience you may want to do it yourself and save. Remember you always pay more for individual-portion boxes of cereal, bags of chips, drink mix packets, and so on.

• Read usage labels and directions. Here are three things to look for: unit pricing and cost per use; double-duty products; and consumer services offered.

Here's an example of what a difference this can make in your dollar value. Take the case of liquid laundry detergent. Let's suppose a 64-oz. bottle of brand X is $3.89, and a 64-oz. bottle of Era Plus is $4.33. If you do simple price comparisons, brand X is cheaper per ounce, so you'd probably buy that brand. However, after reading the directions you'd notice brand X requires 1/2 cup of liquid per use while Era Plus uses only 1/4 cup of liquid per use. That means the bottle of Era Plus will last twice as long as an equal-size bottle of the less concentrated half-cup liquid. So, it's actually a better value.

Woman's Day magazine uses this example. Let's say chuck steak is $2.49 a pound (there are two one-half servings per pound) and flank steak is $3.29 a pound (four servings per pound). The flank figures to be the better value. So, cost per use or serving is an important consideration.

Reading the usage labels indicates what else, if anything, the product can be used for. Citing Era Plus again, it's a pretreater as well as a through-the-wash detergent, so it's a double duty item. There's no sense buying two separate products when one product will do both jobs.

Era Plus provides me with another good example of the third point: consumer services. Like many products on the shelves today, there's a toll-free telephone number printed on the label. If you have a question or a comment about the product, it's a simple matter to dial the consumer hotline. Manufacturers know that the more you understand about their product, the greater your value.

- If the price difference between egg sizes is less than seven cents, the larger eggs are the better buy.

- Watch for day-old specials in the bakery section of the store. Also, the meat counter will frequently sell meat half-price when it's close to its expiration date. The meat is still good quality; just be sure to prepare it shortly after purchase.

- Buy the largest quantity of anything. It's usually cheaper that way *if* you can use it all. Waste is always expensive.

- Any produce sold by the piece (lettuce, two heads for $1; honeydew melon, $1.99 each; pints of strawberries, etc.) should be weighed, and always buy the heaviest portion.

- Don't buy a better grade of product than you need. Flaked tuna is perfect for tuna sandwiches. There's no sense paying more for the large chunk or fancy albacore variety. Grade B (usually broken pieces) of fruits and vegetables are fine when they're going to be chopped in a salad or casserole.

- Check open codes on perishable products to make sure you're getting the freshest goods possible. A few years ago we bought a batch of canned biscuits. They were such a great bargain we picked up one tube after another. While eating them, however, we noticed they had the relative density of manhole covers. I checked the dated cans and they were just that—dated! They had lived a long, though hardly useful life, well beyond the stamped expiration date.

- To monitor your spending, shop with a calculator or plastic purse adder. Knowing your running total may help stave off impulse buying.

- Watch the checker and make sure you are charged the correct amount for your groceries. Stores with "scanners"are a real boon to penny-wise shoppers. These computer registers spit out an itemized list of the products you buy and how much you were charged for each item.

- If you travel a distance to reach a grocery store, an insulated beach bag or styrofoam ice chest keeps frozen foods cold until you get back home. (Some people always keep a plastic milk jug filled with water in their freezers, and when they go shopping on hot days, they put the frozen jug in the foam cooler.)

- If you walk to the market pulling a shopping cart, keep a plastic tablecloth inside. Should it start to rain, you'll have a way to protect your purchases. A cardboard box in the bottom of the cart will keep the grocery bags dry and clean.

- A bicycle basket attached to the wall next to the back door is a handy rack for a bag of groceries while you unlock or open the door.

- Using a collapsible shopping cart is a convenient way to get the groceries from the car to the kitchen in one trip.

See—you survived the cartpushers' game after all. Just follow the rules and you'll be a cinch to win. Though the President might not dial up your "locker room" or invite you to the White House as he does the World Series and National Spelling Bee champs, you'll be a winner just the same. The prize? Extra cash, more free time, and the confidence and skill to become the Sorceress of Safeway!

chapter **8**

THE ONE-MINUTE GOURMET

Ok. So I lied. None of these recipes takes only one minute to prepare, but they're all fast, guaranteed! Some are quick from start to finish, while others are fast to put together but require longer unattended cooking times. A few recipes, such as Easy Lasagne and Applesauce Chip Cake, require a little more time, but they're faster than most "from scratch" recipes. Above all—Enjoy!

HAWAIIAN CHICKEN

4 to 6 chicken breasts
2 cups barbecue sauce
1 16-oz. can crushed pineapple with juice

Preheat oven to 400°F. Place chicken in greased or sprayed baking dish. Bake chicken breasts for 45 minutes. Meanwhile, mix barbecue sauce, pineapple, and juice. Pour mixture over chicken and cook 15 minutes longer. Serves 4 to 6.

CHICKEN REUBEN

8 chicken breasts, boned
salt and pepper to taste

1 16-oz. can sauerkraut
8 slices Swiss cheese
Thousand Island dressing

Preheat oven to 325°F. Put the breasts in a greased or sprayed baking pan. Sprinkle with salt and pepper, if desired. Top with sauerkraut and Swiss cheese. Pour dressing evenly over cheese. Cover pan with foil and bake for 1½ hours. Serves 8. (This is incredibly good—much better than it sounds.)

CHICKEN AND CHEESE SANDWICH

2 5-oz. cans chunk chicken
1 cup chopped raw spinach
1 cup grated cheese
2 English muffins, split and toasted
4 slices onion
2 tablespoons milk
1 egg, beaten
½ teaspoon mustard

Preheat oven to 450°F. Drain chicken, reserving broth. Mix chicken, spinach, and ¼ cup cheese. Top each muffin with onion and one fourth of the chicken mixture. Mix broth and milk. Combine with remaining cheese, egg, and mustard. Spoon over chicken. Bake 5 minutes. Serve at once. Serves 2 to 4.

Dovetailing: Chop spinach, grate cheese, slice onions, and toast muffins in advance.

CHEESY FISH FILLETS

1 16-oz. package frozen fish fillets, thawed
pepper to taste
2 tablespoons butter or margarine
1 12-oz. can frozen condensed cream of shrimp soup, thawed
¼ cup shredded Parmesan cheese
paprika

Preheat oven to 400°F. Grease or spray a nine-inch square baking pan with vegetable cooking spray. Arrange fish in pan. Sprinkle fish with pepper and dot with butter. Pour soup over all. Top with Parmesan cheese and paprika. Bake for 25 minutes. Serves 4.

FISH OR CHICKEN IN FOIL

1 lb. fish fillets cut into four serving-size portions (or substitute four servings of chicken)
salt and pepper, to taste
2 large carrots, thinly sliced
1 zucchini squash, thinly sliced
½ cup water, divided

Preheat oven to 450°F. Place each fish portion in the center of a piece of aluminum foil. Season to taste. Place vegetables and 2 tablespoons of water on top of each. Fold foil over and seal securely on all sides. Place the foil meals in a large baking pan and bake for 18 minutes. Serves 4. Variations: Any thinly sliced vegetables may be substituted for the carrots and zucchini.

Dovetailing: Prepare vegetables ahead. If using chicken, remove bones in advance, too.

ZESTY FISH FILLETS

1 lb. fish fillets
2 tablespoons Worcestershire sauce
1 tablespoon lemon juice
salt and pepper, to taste
½ cup dry bread crumbs

Preheat oven to 500°F. Grease a shallow baking pan. Cut fish into serving size pieces. Combine Worcestershire sauce and lemon juice and dip fish into mixture. Season with salt and pepper and coat with bread crumbs. Bake for 15 minutes. Serves 4.

STEAK SUPPER IN FOIL

1 1½-lb chuck steak (1 inch thick)
1 envelope dry onion soup mix
3 to 4 carrots, sliced

3 potatoes, scrubbed and sliced (leave skins on)
2 tablespoons butter, optional
½ teaspoon salt

Preheat oven to 450°F. Place steak in center of large piece of heavy-duty aluminum foil. Sprinkle soup mix on steak, cover with vegetables. Dot with butter and sprinkle salt overall. Seal dinner carefully in foil. Place on baking sheet. Bake 1 to 1½ hours. Serves 4.

CROCK POT ROUND STEAK AND GRAVY

2 to 2½ lbs. round steak
1 envelope dry onion soup mix
¼ cup water
1 10¾-oz. can cream of mushroom soup

Cut steak into 5 or 6 serving-size pieces, removing fat and bone. Place in crock pot. Add remaining ingredients. Cover and cook on low setting 8 hours or until meat is tender. The gravy is good with potatoes or rice. Serves 5 or 6.

CROCK POT POT ROAST

3 to 4 lbs. beef pot roast
salt and pepper, to taste
1 10¾-oz can vegetable soup, undiluted
½ cup water or tomato juice
⅛ teaspoon dried basil
1 teaspoon dried parsley (or 2 tablespoons fresh)

Season beef with salt and pepper. Place in crock pot. In mixing bowl combine soup, water, and basil. Cover and cook on low setting 10 hours or until meat is tender. Sprinkle with parsley. Makes 6 to 8 servings.

BASIC GROUND BEEF (A quick start to any recipe calling for browned hamburger.)

6 lbs. ground beef

2 cups chopped onions (more or less to taste)

In large Dutch oven brown hamburger and onion. Drain. Divide into six portions and freeze.

Variations: Chopped celery or green pepper may also be added.

EASY LASAGNE

1½ lbs. ground beef
2 tablespoons dried onion (or one onion chopped fine)
1 16-oz. can tomatoes
2 6-oz. cans tomato paste
1 teaspoon salt
¾ teaspoon pepper
½ teaspoon dried oregano
½ teaspoon dried sweet basil
⅛ teaspoon garlic salt
6 to 9 lasagne noodles, cooked
2 cups cottage cheese
8 oz. Swiss cheese
Parmesan cheese

Preheat oven to 350°F. Brown ground beef and onion. Drain fat and add tomatoes, tomato paste, and spices. Simmer for 10 minutes. Arrange noodles in a 9 in. x 10 in. baking pan, in layers with Swiss cheese, cottage cheese, then meat. Repeat once more. Sprinkle generously with Parmesan cheese. Bake for 30 minutes. Serves 8 to 10.

Dovetailing: Using basic ground beef (thawed) cuts 5 minutes off this recipe and eliminates 5 minutes of clean-up time! This recipe can be assembled a day ahead and refrigerated. Bake refrigerated lasagne 45 minutes instead of 30.

LAYERED CASSEROLE

1 large onion, sliced
1 lb. extra-lean ground beef, uncooked
5 medium potatoes, scrubbed and sliced (leave skins on)
1 lb. frozen or canned corn

1 10¾-oz. can cream of mushroom soup

Preheat oven to 375°F. Spray a 9 in. x 13 in. baking pan with vegetable cooking spray. Layer onions, crumbled bround beef, potatoes, corn, and soup. Cover with foil and bake for 1½ hours. Serves 8.

Dovetailing: Slice onion in advance and place in airtight jar. Slice potatoes and cover with water. Drain and dry before using.

SKILLET PORK CHOPS AND RICE

6 pork chops
salt and pepper, to taste
1 cup raw rice
2 cups boiling water
1 envelope dry onion soup mix

Season chops with salt and pepper and brown in skillet. Sprinkle rice around chops. Combine boiling water and soup. Pour over chops and rice. Cover skillet, reduce heat, and simmer until rice is tender and chops are not pink, approximately 45 minutes. Serves 4 to 6.

OVEN-STEAMED RICE

3½ cups boiling water
2 tablespoons butter
1½ teaspoon salt
dash pepper
1½ cups raw rice

Preheat oven to 350°F. Combine all ingredients in a 1½ quart oven-proof casserole dish. Cover tightly with foil and bake for 45 minutes. Serves 6 to 8.

Dovetailing: Whenever you turn on your oven, check the upcoming week's menu plans. If you'll need rice sometime during the week, bake it now and reheat as needed.

QUESADILLAS

8 corn tortillas
1 to 2 cups grated Jack cheese
1 cup alfalfa sprouts
2 cups chopped tomatoes
½ cup chopped green onions
1 cup chopped avocados
sour cream

Preheat oven to 500°F. Grease or spray a large cookie sheet. Place tortillas on baking sheet and cover generously with cheese. Bake until cheese is melted. Remove from oven and top with desired toppings. Serves 8. Serve with rice or refried beans.

Dovetailing: Grate cheese and chop vegetables in advance.

WHOLE WHEAT SALAD

1 cup whole wheat kernels
1 cup chopped celery
½ cup sliced radishes
½ cup sliced green onions
1 4-6 oz. can shrimp, drained
salt, to taste
mayonnaise, to taste

Place wheat kernels in saucepan and cover with water. Soak wheat overnight. Drain water and cover wheat with fresh water. Boil for 20 to 30 minutes. Drain wheat and cool. Toss wheat with remaining ingredients. Serves 8.

Variations: Add peas, chopped green pepper, sliced olives, or diced pimento.

Dovetailing: Wheat and vegetables can be prepared ahead.

ITALIAN SALAD

12 oz. marinated artichoke hearts, drained

18 cherry tomatoes, cut in half
1 3-oz. can sliced mushrooms, drained
2 3-oz. cans chopped black olives, drained

Toss ingredients together. Serve on spinach leaves. Pass vinegar and oil dressing.

BROCCOLI HOLLANDAISE

2 10-oz. packages frozen broccoli (spears or chopped)
1/2 cup sour cream
1/2 cup mayonnaise
1 teaspoon mustard
2 teaspoons lemon juice

Cook broccoli according to package directions. Meanwhile, combine remaining ingredients in saucepan and cook just until heated. Serve sauce over broccoli. Serves 6 to 8.

QUICK FRUIT SALAD

1 3½-oz. package instant vanilla pudding
2 1-lb. cans fruit cocktail, drained but reserve the juice
1 cup miniature marshmallows
1 cup coconut, optional
3 bananas, sliced

Thicken pudding in reserved juice. Blend until smooth. Fold in remaining ingredients. Chill until thickened. Serves 6 to 8.

ONE-CUP SALAD

1 cup sour cream
1 cup Mandarin oranges, drained
1 cup pineapple chunks, drained
1 cup miniature marshmallows
1 cup coconut

Combine all ingredients. Chill. Serves 6.

CHOCOLATE PIE

1 8-oz. chocolate bar (with or without almonds)
1 12-oz. container whipped topping, thawed
1 9-in. chocolate cookie pie crust

In top of double boiler (or in microwave), melt chocolate bar. Cool slightly and fold into whipped topping. Pour into crust and chill. Serves 6 to 8.

BLENDER LEMONADE PIE

1 6-oz. can frozen lemonade concentrate
¼ cup lemon juice (fresh is best)
1 14-oz. can sweetened condensed milk (NOT evaporated milk)
1 12-oz. container whipped topping, thawed
1 graham cracker crust

Combine lemonade, juice, and milk in blender. Fold into whipped topping and pour into pie crust. Chill until set. Serves 6 to 8.

QUICK JELL-O PIE

vanilla wafers
1 3-oz. package strawberry Jell-O
¾ cup boiling water
10 oz. frozen strawberries
2 cups strawberry ice cream

Line bottom and sides of an 8-inch pie pan with whole vanilla wafers. Dissolve Jell-O in ¾ cup boiling water. Stir in sliced strawberries. Stir until fruit thaws and separates. If necessary, chill until Jell-O is slightly thickened. Add ice cream and blend with electric mixer until smooth. Pour into pie shell. Chill until firm. Serves 6.

Variations: Increase boiling water to 1½ cups and omit frozen strawberries. Combine vanilla ice cream with any flavor gelatin.

APPLESAUCE CHOCOLATE CHIP CAKE *(quickest "from scratch" cake you can make)*

½ cup shortening
1½ cup sugar
2 eggs
2 tablespoons baking cocoa
1 cup applesauce
2 cups flour
½ teaspoon baking soda
1 teaspoon baking powder
½ teaspoon salt
½ teaspoon cinnamon
2 tablespoons sugar
1 cup chocolate chips

Preheat oven to 350°F. Grease and flour a 9 in. x 13 in. baking pan. Cream shortening, 1½ cups sugar, and eggs. Add applesauce and dry ingredients, mixing well. Pour into prepared baking pan. Sprinkle 2 tablespoons sugar and the chocolate chips on top of batter. Bake 35 minutes. Serves 6 to 8. Note: For high altitudes, omit baking powder.

CARAMEL CRUMBALLS

caramel ice cream topping
caramel cashew ice cream
cookie crumbs

Pour about 3 tablespoons of syrup into individual ice-cream dishes. Scoop and form balls of ice cream and roll in cookie crumbs. Place each crumball on top of syrup in ice-cream dishes. Serve immediately.

Dovetailing: Form ice-cream balls in advance, roll in crumbs and freeze.

Nothing perks up interest in cooking more than new and delicious recipes. Give some of these quickies a try and escape from that kitchen!

chapter 9

MAKING A CLEAN SWEEP

You name it, I've cleaned it. Oh, I've had the usual kitchen messes to contend with, like corn flakes welded to cereal bowls, but I've also had my share of humdingers. Like the time I made up a five-gallon batch of Kool-Aid. No big deal, you say? Just wait. I poured the water, sugar, (and plenty of it) and punch mix into a large insulated jug, and reached into the drawer below for a long-handled stirring spoon. Just then, the phone rang so I scurried to answer it, leaving the drawer open. Meanwhile, back in the kitchen, the dye was cast—literally.

The jug's spigot was open, so Kool-Aid was filling up the opened drawer, dripping into the cupboard underneath and streaming onto the kitchen floor, much to the delight of a neighboring colony of ants. (Organized, but dumb, you say?)

Now, sixteen years, 17,000 meals, and as many (or more) messes later I figure I know just a little about cleaning kitchens. Basically, cleaning up a kitchen is a three-step process: (would that it only took three steps!)

Prevent
Schedule
Do

My first consideration in saving time is to prevent the work in the first place. Here are some prevention tricks I use in my kitchen. Even trying just a few of the ideas will cut a real swath in the time you normally spend in cleaning up.

KEEP OUT DIRT

Stop the dirt where it starts—at the entrances to your home. Door mats keep your house cleaner, and reduce the need for shampooing, waxing, washing floors, and floor coverings. According to America's only living Mr. Clean, Don Aslett (author of *Is There Life After Housework?*) "Proper matting alone can save the average household approximately 200 hours of work a year, slow down structure depreciation, and save over $100 in direct cleaning supply costs."

Avoid using carpet remnants, mats with cloth backing, link or perforated mats. They just don't do the job of removing all the dust, dirt, fine gravel, and grit that hangs onto incoming shoes. Don recommends commercial nylon-tuft mats inside the door and synthetic grass or rough textured mats outside. They should be long enough to allow four steps on each. These mats may be purchased from a janitorial supply house or by mail. For more information and a free catalogue write to: Housework, Inc., P.O. Box 39, Pocatello, Idaho 83204.

In the meantime, start training your family to leave their shoes at the door. I have a wonderfully organized friend who has been very successful with that tactic. Actually, any fact associated with home management and efficiency Sherrill can spit out as if she were a dot matrix printer. She keeps restaurant-sized dishpans just inside the front and back doors. Before the children come into the house, they slip off their shoes, toss them into the dishpan and enter the house. She has them so well trained they are never in the house with their shoes on. Each family member's shoes, by the way, are stored in large restaurant-sized dishpans on shelves in the attached garage.

Sherrill's children are no different from your kids or my kids. The difference is Sherrill. She is consistent and her training is reflected in her family's willingness to cooperate. (Get this: she has single-handle faucets in her house and everyone turns them off with their elbows so the chrome stays drip-free.) Perhaps you think that's going a bit too far, but Sherrill has indeed learned the time-saving value of prevention. I've never met anyone who accomplishes so much; even with a full-time job, she still has free time for hobbies, entertaining, family, and friends.

Another friend of ours has an engraved brass plaque on her front door that politely asks all visitors to remove their shoes. And yes, I always wear my good socks when I go over to her house.

Although a good share of house dirt is tracked in with the shoes, still more soot is coming in through poorly insulated doors and windows. Seal those openings. Keep furnace and air-conditioning filters and vents serviced regularly. Keep dirty (I mean d-i-r-t-y) clothes, boots, shoes, and toys outside. Empty the vacuum bag frequently so it won't spew dust around the house when you use it.

3 A'S FOR CLEANING WHILE YOU COOK

Every time you make sandwiches, soup, or a gourmet feast, always perform the three high *A*'s of meal preparation:

1. Fill the sink with hot, soapy water.
2. Spread a sheet of freezer wrap on the counter.
3. Put a temporary trash container on the floor by the center you're working at.

Nothing speeds up kitchen work quite like cleaning as you go. Do your preparations on the freezer wrap (it's waxed on one side) to keep the counter clean and free of splatters. When you're finished with a utensil, toss it in the sink of soapy water. Wipe up spills as you go, so you won't have to scrub later. Having the trash container handy will encourage you to discard opened cans, wrappers, and empty jars instead of just keeping them on the counter "for now" until you clean up the kitchen.

Aside from the obvious benefits, the real advantage of the three *A*'s is that you approach your work in an organized manner. With these three visual reminders, you automatically do things more efficiently because you're *thinking* more efficiently.

DO IT NOW

Replace things immediately when you see they've been put away in the wrong spot. Stanislaus Leszczynski said, "No snowflake in an avalanche ever feels responsible." Melt the snowflake before it has a chance to become an avalanche. Here are some specific ideas.

After using the oven, wipe it out before it completely cools down. You'll save hours of work by eliminating the eventual soldered mass. Clean your range top and drip pans daily for the same reason.

Wipe off bottles, jars, canisters, etc., before you put them away; likewise small appliances; don't put anything away unless it's clean and in good repair.

WATCH THE CLOCK

I never realized just how long a minute was until we got a microwave. Steaming a hot dog for fifty seconds sometimes seems like forever!

When I was a national spokesperson for Procter and Gamble, several times I had to appear on noon news programs and had only a minute and a half to deliver my message. No problem. My microwave taught me that you can say and do a lot in one minute.

When I realized I could empty the dishwasher in less time than one commercial break, I didn't loathe the job quite so much. The same goes for watering the kitchen plants, washing the kitchen sink window and appliance doors. My point is this: if you think there's just too much to do and no time to do it; if you actually abominate a particular job or jobs, find out just how much time the task takes. More than likely it's a fraction of what you imagine it to be; thus, it becomes more palatable.

Another way time figures in a clean kitchen is to budget it correctly. Include clean-up time with the time it takes to make something. In other words, if you want to throw a casserole together before you leave for work, give yourself enough time to get the meal preparations cleaned up. too. (Whenever possible, that is.)

THE KITCHEN IS CLOSED

When you're watching TV and the picture gets a little fuzzy, what happens? Sure, the little man inside the TV holds up a sign that says, "Video difficulties. Please stand by."

When you go to a store that's being remodeled, what does the management tell us? "Pardon our dust. We're remodeling to serve you better."

And when you travel cross-country and the highway is ripped

up, the road warriors make it okay by saying, "Road construction next 97 miles. Thank you for your cooperation."

We go along with all these excuses simply because we have no other choice. So, I figured why not do the same at home? Closing the kitchen at a certain time every night (and sticking to the rule) is a great way to keep your kitchen clean. (Admittedly this is easier if you have young children and no one working the swing shift.) Ideally, this hour should be a half hour before bed, so while the kids are getting ready, I can once and for all put the finishing touches on the kitchen knowing it will stay that way until morning.

Anyone who can't abide by this system should take an oath (similar to the one taken by adopters of Cabbage Patch Kids) that they will clean up all signs of meal preparations before they go to bed. If you're feeling especially mean you can insist they arise early in the morning to take care of anything they neglected.

That's the textbook method for closing your kitchen. Here's how we do it. I'll say something like this, "The kitchen is closing in thirty minutes. If you're going to eat anything, do it now." We don't necessarily have a regular time every night, either. I just go with my particular mood that day. (Forgive me, Dr. Spock.) After the thirty minutes (or whatever) has passed, the person in charge of the kitchen puts it to sleep for the night.

That takes care of preventive maintenance in the kitchen. You can see how, with very little effort, hours of work, worry, and frustration are excised from KP duty. Next step: schedule.

THE SCHEDULE OF EVENTS— YOUR CLEANING SCHEDULE

Some time ago I was flying out of town to appear on "Hour Magazine." Before I boarded the plane I made a quick stop in the airport bathroom and happened to notice a cleaning schedule that was hanging on the wall. It included three columns:

Column One: Each specific job was listed.

Column Two: A space to record the date and time the job was completed.

Column Three: The initials of the person who performed the job.

The whole system was so well-organized that even one with a good deal of aspic in her brain cells would know exactly what to do. I wondered why it was necessary to have everything spelled out. These janitors are intelligent, hard-working people. Certainly they can clean up an airport bathroom and do a good job of it. Don Aslett answered my question.

Don, in addition to authoring the books I mentioned, is president of Varsity Contractors, one of the largest janitorial service companies in the world. He told me that before any of their jobs are contracted, everyone knows exactly what jobs will be done, how long it will take, when and how often each task will be completed. He pointed out that in industry where profits are made and lost, scheduling—even in such detail as the airport bathroom—is necessary in order to get the work done faster, better, and at less expense.

I'm convinced we should take the same approach at home. Certainly, we, too, want to do things better, faster, and at less ex-

DAILY	M	T	W	T	F	S	S
Do Dishes							
Wipe Off and Put Away Appliances							
Wipe Off Table and Chairs							
Clean Countertop							
Clean Stove Top							
Wash Drip Pans							
Wipe Out Warm Oven (if used)							
Wipe Off Appliance Doors							
Dust Top of Refrigerator							
Sweep Floor							
Mop Floor, If Needed							
Empty Trash							
Clean Sink and Drain Trap							
Polish Fixtures							

pense. (I'd just settle for faster!)

I was so inspired by the airport form that I drew one up and photocopied a stack for our family to use. Now, anyone who's old enough to read knows exactly what has to be done on a day-to-day basis. If one child is assigned kitchen work for a whole week, hang up the chart as is (making changes as you deem necessary) and tell him to initial each job when it's completed. Tell him the weekly chores on the bottom of the form need to be done only once before the week is finished. He can decide when to do those, or you can specify a day.

An alternative is to put the initials of the person responsible in the appropriate box and have that person check it off when he's completed each assignment. In addition to this daily/weekly form, you may want to make one for monthly and semiannual jobs.

Schedules see to it that a job isn't neglected longer than it

WEEKLY

Wipe Off Switches, Outlets		*Clean Phone*	
Wipe Off Doorknobs		*Remove Cobwebs*	
Wipe Off Cupbd. Doors, Handles		*Dust Shelves, Figurines, Wall Decorations*	
Wipe Off Windowsills		*Dust Door Ledges*	
Clean Vents		*Dust Hanging Lights*	
Clean Canisters		*Spot Wash Walls*	
Wash Sink Window		*Mop Floors, Baseboards*	
Wash Sliding Glass Door		*Wipe Off Shelves & Drawers Where Crumbs Have Accum.*	
Clean Range Hood		*Clean Microwave*	

should be, which only increases the amount of time it takes to do it. Schedules prevent you from wasting time doing things more often than is necessary. With a written schedule you never have to make the decision, "What should I do next?" Aside from that, a written schedule lists in black and white exactly what needs to be done so everyone can help. With a physical list, even a drop-in visitor would know what to do.

The whole purpose of a schedule is to help you get the most out of what time, energy, and money you have available—vital issues in today's busy world.

When determining your schedule, approach it with a questioning attitude:

Is this job necessary? If so, why?

Can I do the job in another way, another time, in another order, or in some other place?

Is it important that *I* do the job, or that the job just gets done?

Is the job appropriate?

Will it influence habits?

Will it make our memories happier or unhappier?

Will it spoil the aesthetic appeal of our home?

Does the job have to be done, or is it just a habit?

Now that we've prevented the need for so many tedious chores and scheduled the rest, all that's left is step number three: DO!

GET IT DONE!

While I hardly, if ever, feel like Mary Poppins when I'm chiseling burnt-on food and grease from the bottom of the electric frying pan, I've learned that a spoonful of sugar does, indeed, help the medicine go down. Here are a few sweet morsels that help me, at least, tolerate kitchen cleanup.

Play some snappy music while you're puttering around in the kitchen. A nice fast piece helps you move along at a steady rhythmic pace. At any rate, have something pleasant going on. ("Read" a classic by means of your cassette tape player; have a special dessert baking in the oven, or visit with a friend.) The whole idea is to have a pleasant association with your work.

Break your jobs down into small, manageable portions, so the entire job won't seem so looming and unconquerable. For regular maintenance, divide cleaning chores into fifteen to twenty minute segments every day, or devote some extra time one day a week. Or, after doing up the dishes, clean out one drawer or one shelf.

To thoroughly clean the kitchen, work in this order: cupboards, range, oven, fans, refrigerator, walls, woodwork, windows, sink, curtains (or window treatments), and floors.

Knowing the direction you're going to take makes breaking down the job much easier. If possible, plan a deep-cleaning session when your schedule isn't too demanding.

Categorize your kitchen chores into *A-B-C* priority. Some *A*'s might be: dishes, countertop, empty trash. *C*'s might include: wipe off doorknobs, dust top of refrigerator, clean canisters. That way if you're ever hit with a crisis (and who isn't from time to time) you'll know what the best use of your time is right now—the *A*'s. The *C*'s can wait, if they have to.

Keep cleaning supplies contained in a plastic cleanup caddy or other tote. Use it to hold your *A*-type cleaning solutions, a few soft rags, a Chore Girl, and perhaps a plastic trash bag. (Chore Girls are those curly stainless steel scrubbers. They're great for quickly removing lumps of hard grease that accumulate on the top and sides of the stove and the sides of the refrigerator, if it's close to the stove.)

For quick cleanups keep your cleaning solutions (neutral cleaner, nontoxic disinfectant, degreaser, and evaporative alcohol-based cleaner) in spray bottles. Be sure you give the chemical a chance to work so you won't have to scrub. Let the solution penetrate and loosen hardened particles and all you'll have to do is wipe them away. (Again I'll refer you to *Is There Life After Housework?* It's the uncontested winner for the "Fastest Cleanup This Side of Red China" award.)

While dirt and grime pose a threat to any kitchen, there's another more obvious type of pest to contend with: clutter. We tend to keep in sight what we want to keep in mind, so the clutter stacks up like cannonballs in a courtyard. And for some strange reason that "courtyard" is usually the kitchen. Coupons, canceled checks, credit card receipts, wrappers, bills, magazines, phone messages, check stubs, school papers, library books, etc. If the kitchen is the heart of the home and all this stuff is "pumped" into

Escape from the Kitchen

it, you could well be in the final stages of cardiac arrest.

The following preventive measures will effect the "coronary bypass surgery" and rid your kitchen of clutter once and for all.

FAMILY ORGANIZER

The family organizer, described in detail in *Confessions II*, is exactly what it claims to be. It's a looseleaf notebook and contains a running telephone log (eliminating all those miscellaneous scraps of floating paper), weekly planning sheets for the kids, directory of frequently called phone numbers (and emergency numbers), sports rosters and schedules, school handbooks, and anything else the family needs to refer to on a regular basis. (Copies of the telephone log and the planning sheets can be found in *Confessions II*.

I demonstrate the family organizer at all my seminars and I've had to make up a "dummy" just for that purpose. You see, our family organizer has become such an important part of our family life, I can never remove it from home! It saves me at least two hours a week because we don't have to hunt for needed information, nor do we have to shuffle, stack, and clean around the clutter. ("Clean around the clutter" is a sister slogan of "ring around the collar," I believe.)

PLANNING NOTEBOOK

For years I've been singing the praises of my planning notebook and, as promised, I'll sing again right now. Whatever floating paper is not obliterated by the family organizer is now put to rest here.

When I see a piece of paper, I decide if it's of general family interest or something that other members of the family will have to refer to. If so, it goes in the family organizer. If some of the details are necessary for me to be aware of, I copy them into my planning notebook (game times, work schedules, school info, etc.). When I receive notices from the PTA listing school days off, early dismissal times, holidays, activities, parent-teacher conferences, etc., I jot down the necessary information in the calendar section of my planning notebook and throw the original notice away. Ditto with wedding, shower, and party invitations, appointment notices, and anything else I'm notified about. The planning notebook, as you can see, has eliminated a lot of paper already—but there's more.

I handle some letters pretty much the same way. I read the letter, put a reminder in my calendar to answer it (I may include a few notes about the letter) then I toss the letter away.

When I'm watching TV or visiting with a friend and hear of a great new recipe to try—you guessed it—it's written in my planner.

If I'm reading an article and discover something I want to send for, the address and other pertinent information is penned in my planning notebook.

My planner houses the shopping list; to-do's; incandescent, though rare, ideas; directions for getting someplace; book notes; meeting agendas; travel itineraries; car mileage; business expenses; in fact, all information that comes to me is recorded in a singular source, my planning notebook. It even boasts autographs from Tiny Tim and Steve Garvey. (Yes girls, he *is* gorgeous!) Since I need a lot of writing room I use the two-pages-per-day Day-Timer.

FILING SYSTEM— APPLIANCE RECORD

There's another type of paper problem consisting of incoming and outgoing mail, coupons, recipes, appliance manuals, receipts, check stubs, and the like. Recipes and coupons were covered in Chapters 7 and 8, so let's zero in on the other stuff.

Every December I buy two expanding files for the upcoming year. One is letter size with twelve pockets (one for each month of the year) and another made especially for cancelled checks. This is a very simple system, and makes filing so easy, it's a snap to keep up on it. Here's how it works.

All cancelled checks, bank statements, and deposit slips are filed by month in the check file. The receipts, paid bills, credit card purchase slips, etc., are filed in the large expanding envelope, also by month. If you ever have to refer to a receipt or check on a credit card purchase, you'll only have a handful of papers to flip through in order to find the one you need. This is much better than setting up a file for each company you do business with, because it eliminates confusion and wasted time. At the end of the year, pull your tax working papers, close up the files and keep stored in a box for a few years. It's fast, easy, and takes up very little room. I also recommend having *one* spot (say a decorative basket, dishpan, or drawer) where all incoming paper is put until it is worked through the system.

It's also smart to keep track of instruction booklets, warranties, and service information on the appliances you purchase. Here are two methods to store them.

I have another letter-sized expanding file with several alphabetized pockets. The refrigerator booklet, receipt, warranty, etc. is simply put in the "R" pocket. The mixer information is placed under M, and so on. I usually keep the instruction booklet right by the appliance until I'm comfortable with and knowledgeable about its operation. Then, the booklet is filed away. This file is used for things in every room of the house (i.e., the kids' record player = R, piano = P, grill = G, care of the drapes = D). I don't waste time alphabetizing any farther than the first letter.

Here's the second method: Each appliance's information is placed in separate vinyl sheet protectors (sack type) and placed alphabetically in a looseleaf notebook.

Using either method, it is helpful to keep an appliance chart (see illustration). This form can be placed in the family organizer, in the expanding file, or in the appliance notebook.

If you're moving and going to leave any appliances in the house, be thoughtful and leave the instruction booklets and any other pertinent information for the new owners.

Errand Drawer

Where do you put things like this: the neighbor boy's Matchbox car, the cassette you borrowed from Marge, the agenda you need to photocopy, the cake plate that belongs to your neighbor, and the broken drawer pull you have to match when you buy a new one? The only logical solution is to pile it up somewhere (usually in the kitchen) so you'll remember to take care of all these little things.

Here's what I do. I make a note in my planning notebook to take care of whatever it is (or I delegate the chore) and put all the paraphernalia into the errand drawer. I'm not going to forget it because it's on my to-do list, but at least it's out of sight and keeping clutter out of my kitchen. If you don't have a drawer to spare, use a cardboard box, tote bag, or Rubbermaid stacking shelf (the ones with drawers are especially practical). Consolidate and conceal this junk and see what it does for your kitchen.

Appliance	Amount Paid	Check Number	Purchase Date	Where Purchased	Model	Serial Number	Service Information	Warranty Period

Plastic stacking bins are useful anywhere you need extra storage.

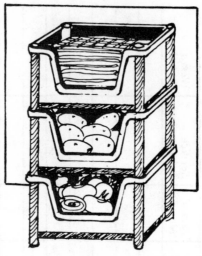

Landing/Launch Pads

These are merely in-out baskets for the kids. When they come home from school, all the debris is tossed in their respective dishpans. Articles they're clipping, books they're reading, lunch money, signed permission slips, etc. all are put into the landing pads and launch them to school the next day with no hassles and no clutter piled club-sandwich-style on the kitchen counter. Cull the dead wood occasionally (corrected spelling tests, old math work, scraps from art projects) to keep the system running smoothly.

You need one container for each child—tote or book bags, stacking bins, drawers, cardboard boxes, dishpans, baskets, etc. are all good choices.

The best place to keep these containers is where the after-school rubble normally lands; loosely translated, that usually means in the kitchen.

Stack bins in a corner or on a closet floor; hang tote bags from a peg; eliminate a few more *C*'s from your kitchen, and open up some shelf space. Wherever you keep them, landing and launch pads will make an arresting improvement in the appearance of your kitchen.

Tool Box

Every self-respecting kitchen needs a tool box. Pan lids will loosen, as well as drawer pulls and door knobs. Decorative objects need to be hung from time to time. (Our eight-year-old, the pizza-powered Jeffrey, is an all-star wrestling fan. He practices drop kicks on any available wall, so I'm hanging, and rehanging, decorative objects quite frequently. A few of them, though, have hit the ground so many times they are no longer decorative.) If your kitchen is the hub around which your house revolves, then a tool box will prove quite handy.

Here's a skeleton list of things to include: claw hammer, Phillips screw driver (one large, one small), flathead screwdrivers (one large, one small), pliers, utility knife, tape measure, tacks, masking tape, wire, hooks, and an assortment of nails, wood screws, nuts, and bolts. Optional items: tack hammer, duct tape, nail set, pipe wrenches, saw, level, sandpaper.

Your tools can be stored in a cardboard box, cleaning caddy, tote bag, drawer, crock, basket, or a small plastic tool box. Be sure to mark each tool so you'll recognize it as belonging in the kitchen. These tools will likely wander because they'll probably be the only ones people can find with any regularity. So don't allow these tools to be removed from the periphery of the kitchen. (Since not allowing people to do something doesn't usually work, mark the gear so you can at least be able to claim it.)

Junk Drawer

Over the years I've written about a lot of home management problems, but I get more flack over the crummy junk drawer. What is a junk drawer? It's a place where you put things you don't know what to do with. Just look at all that stuff:

Batteries—the last time you used them in your tape player, Beverly Sills sounded more like Tennessee Ernie Ford. So you bought fresh batteries. These old ones were thrown in the junk drawer because they still had a little juice in them. Or, you bought a four pack and only needed two, so the extras were tossed in the drawer. Why not throw away those slow-motion batteries immediately and store the new ones by the appliance they'll be used with?

And what about the rope, tangles of wire, broken sunglasses, buttons, paperclips, shredded cassette tape (as soon as you have a few minutes you're going to rewind it, right?) unidentified keys, rawhide bones, and used aluminum foil? Designate the junk drawer as a mini office center (for pens, pencils, stapler, staples, scissors, scratch pad, eraser, paperclips, tacks, tape, etc.) then **C-C-C** it.

Tools or hardware-type things go in the tool box. Buttons go with mending equipment. Things you've "been gonna" fix for over a year are discarded. If you have several fixits in the junk drawer, make a note in your planner to fix each item, and store the projects in a box (and don't keep the box in the kitchen). Now that you know about prioritizing and storing at the point of first use, the junk drawer will be easier to dismantle.

Phone Cord

Purchase the longest telephone cord you can find. (The phone company can special-order a 25-foot one, or pick one up at Radio Shack.) My superwoman friend, Sherrill, even scrubs her floor while talking on the phone. As a matter of fact, she's the one who converted me. I never talk to her but what she's doing something—washing dishes, watering plants, sealing her ceramic tile countertop. Only a long phone cord (or better yet a cordless phone) will allow you to talk and work at the same time. Buy a shoulder cradle or self-adhesive phone cushion—wherever they sell phones. That'll make the talk/work combination more comfortable.

Dishes? Toss 'em in the Trash

Even in kitchens with dishwashers there are always dishes piled in the sink, sprinkled across the countertop, stacked on the table, or piled on top of any horizontal surface. The problem is that often the dishwasher is filled with clean dishes, and besides, no red-blooded American kid is going to take the time to check out whether the dishes are clean or dirty. Here's a solution, whether you have a dishwasher or not.

Keep a tall plastic wastebasket or restaurant-sized dishpan under the sink. When a dish is used, teach everyone to *scrape and rinse* it off and place it in the wastebasket. When it's time to wash the dishes or load the dishwasher, just empty the wastebasket and begin. Using this method your kitchen will always look fairly neat. Just be sure the dishes are done at least once a day!

If you don't have room under your sink, there's a decorative idea: purchase a pretty wicker clothes hamper with a lid and buy a plastic wastebasket to fit inside. The hamper can be anywhere, yet it'll conceal the dishes (or trash) you're keeping inside it.

To cut down on the number of cups and glasses you need to wash, here's a great hint. Buy a large, colored mug for each member of the family. (Each person has a different color.) During the day, whenever anyone wants to drink something he uses his own mug instead of reaching into the cupboard for a clean glass. We keep our mugs in a dishpan under the sink. After each use, we rinse them out and put them back into the dishpan. Or, hang the mugs on hooks inside the sink cupboard door. Once a day, the mugs are washed with hot, soapy water.

This one idea alone has been a tremendous time and clutter saver!

NITTY GRITTY NOTES

- Divide cupboards into three, four, or five sections and clean one section a day (or every other day). By the end of a week (or two) the cupboards are clean.

- Instead of regular shelf paper, try using freezer wrap. The tear-off box makes it easy to dispense just the right length.

- For cupboards not flush with the ceiling, cover with plastic wrap, foil, or freezer wrap. It can't be seen and will keep you from having to clean off the eventual greasy buildup.

- If you have kitchen carpeting, attach a small bag to the vacuum to hold the stray buttons, coins, toys, pins, etc. that you discover while vacuuming. I also put things in the bag that my vacuum won't pick up: dried palm fronds, wrappers stuck to the carpet, and big chunks of anything.

- A small whisk broom hung on the vacuum is handy to use in corners or other small crevices the vacuum head can't reach.

- An old toothbrush helps you clean between and around appliance buttons, can-opener parts, faucets, tines of forks, graters, and strainers.

- A percolator brush is useful to clean the crumbs from the toaster. (Unplug the toaster first!)

- Before cleaning appliances, always refer to the manufacturer's instruction manual. If no booklet is available, check the nameplate on the appliance to determine the model number (or simply take a picture of the appliance). Send this information to the manufacturer along with your request for a new manual. If you don't have the manufacturer's address, call your local appliance dealer. He can give it to you.

• A long handled windshield brush is perfect for retrieving stray pieces of food from underneath the stove or refrigerator and also reaches between large appliances.

• Secure a damp sponge (or old stocking) to the end of a yardstick to swish under appliances or to dust hard-to-reach refrigerator coils.

• Soak and dissolve is still the easiest way, but a plastic windshield ice scraper is good for prying loose dried-on foods from the floor, table, counter, etc. if you're impatient.

• An old, but clean, mascara brush or a percolator brush is great for cleaning window tracks.

• Whenever you wash something (floors, counters, appliances), always rinse and buff dry, even if the product says, "No rinsing necessary."

• Clean out the refrigerator on garbage collection day if you have no food disposer. (Or freeze the unwanted food until garbage day.) That way, you'll eliminate smelly trash and discourage neighborhood pets.

• Sponges, plastic scrubbers, and dish mops will be clean and fresh-smelling if you occasionally clean them on the top rack of the dishwasher.

• Before broiling, put a few cups of water in the bottom of the broiler pan. You won't believe how easy it'll be to clean.

• To clean oven racks, spread a bath towel in the bathtub, place the racks on top and cover with hot water. Add ammonia and let soak.

• When mixing juice, Kool-Aid, etc., or when pouring anything, do it in the sink (or cover the counter with a paper towel or freezer wrap.)

• Store small amounts of leftovers in microwave-safe paper cups. Good for heating leftovers in the microwave without dirtying dishes.

• A lockable, portable metal file box is a good clean-up caddy for families with young children.

• Molded plastic high chairs are easy to clean in the shower. Remove any fabric pads, then spray on the hot water. Give it a chance to penetrate and loosen the cement-like globs, then wash clean, and dry.

- Spread newspapers down under the high chair or under a small child's chair before every meal.

- To keep pet dishes in place, put a rubber jar ring underneath or use a baby suction-cup cereal dish. Or keep a placemat, towel, or bathroom mat under the dishes to catch drips.

- A hanging purse file holds more than purses. It provides hanging storage for phone books, file folders, paper bags, boxes of wraps and foil, incoming and outgoing mail, magazines, etc.

- Do you have slits in your vinyl kitchen chairs? Cover them with bathtub appliques.

- For ceramic tile countertops, seal once a year with Red Devil Tile and Grout Sealer. Just follow the manufacturer's directions. My friend Sherrill does this religiously and her six-year-old kitchen still looks brand new!

- When you want the kitchen to smell like you've been home all day working feverishly (and you haven't) put some orange peelings in a 350°F. oven.

In your fight against grime, keep your eye out for dust catchers and dirt carriers and eliminate work at the outset. Reduce clutter by enlisting some of the methods I introduced earlier.

Be objective and view your kitchen as a visitor would. What looks unkempt, cluttered, dirty, or worn out? Make a list and work on trouble spots one at a time. Before long your kitchen will be a place of refuge, not a place for refuse!

chapter 10

THAT'S ENTER- TAINMENT

There are those who think a party is not worth throwing unless it's done right: twinkle lights in the trees; three forks (and as many spoons) per place setting; tablecloths, china, flowers, hostess' gown carefully coordinated with the color of the wallcoverings; the tinkle of a baby grand piano—all the while giving careful attention to every nuance of taste and texture of the catered fare.

Folks who run in those circles are not a part of the audience I'm meaning to help. I'm after those who would just like to find time to entertain a few friends without throwing your back out. Never mind if your house is thick with dust and thin on amenities, or you wince at the thought of your lackluster recipe collection. The most important ingredient for a successful party besides a congenial group of people is a list.

We all know someone who can throw a great bash with seemingly little effort. Her house can be as crowded as the freeway at rush hour yet she mingles with her guests with the grace and unhurried poise of Vanna White demonstrating prizes on "Wheel of Fortune."

How does she do it? Planning. The more casual and effortless it seems, the more planning has usually gone into it. Good planning eliminates any last minute problems, making the event more enjoyable for the hostess and her guests.

The first question you need to ask is, "How many?" The number of guests you plan to invite influences the other things you need to consider (type of party, budget, etc.). If you're going to invite six people, a sit-down dinner is feasible. A group of twenty-five, however, might be better served by a buffet, cocktail party, or an outdoor barbecue, for example.

Once you've arrived at a figure, think about the following:

- How much money do you want to spend? Again, this will have a bearing on the type of party you choose.
- Are you planning a party for a special occasion (birthday, housewarming, holiday) or is it just a get-together?
- Will your house comfortably accommodate this many people? How much activity will your kitchen (ovens, refrigerator, etc.) handle?
- Do you have enough equipment for a group this large? (Place settings, tables, chairs, linens, etc.). If not, what will you need to rent or borrow? If renting, will it fit into your budget?
- If you have children, where will they be, or how will they be cared for?

Once you've digested this information you're ready to do some hard core planning:

- Who will be invited?
- Date and time of party?
- Type of party?
- Menu

On page 155 you'll find a copy of my party planner. I don't have time to forget anything so I write everything down. After the event, I put these copies in an entertainment file, which makes short work of future party-planning sessions.

The party planner is your timetable and constant reminder before the party actually starts. At the top of the sheet, jot down the number of guests, type of party, and date, in the appropriate spaces. Then, as you plan the menu, jot down each item in the menu section. (When the dish is actually completed, put a check mark by it.)

As you list each food item, jot down all the equipment you'll need for its service. Do you have an ovenproof dish that's big enough? Is there plenty of room in your refrigerator for all those salads? Portable toaster ovens, crock pots, electric fry pans, and

PARTY PLANNER

DATE _____ *NO. OF GUESTS* _____ *TYPE OF PARTY* _____

Menu:

___ _____   ___ _____
___ _____   ___ _____
___ _____   ___ _____
___ _____   ___ _____
___ _____   ___ _____

Equipment	Shopping List	Amount
___ _____	___ _____	
___ _____	___ _____	
___ _____	___ _____	
___ _____	___ _____	
___ _____	___ _____	
___ _____	___ _____	
___ _____	___ _____	
___ _____	___ _____	
Miscellaneous To Do	___ _____	
___ _____	___ _____	
___ _____	___ _____	
___ _____	___ _____	
___ _____	___ _____	

microwaves can expand your oven space and insulated ice chests can keep several small items cold. Perhaps a neighbor will let you store some of the overflow in her refrigerator or heat something in her oven.

Next, list all the necessary ingredients (and the amounts) to make each dish. If the equipment or food is on hand put a check mark by it. If not, the unchecked items will remind you that they need to be taken care of. Anything you need to purchase (ice, candles, special napkins, coasters, etc.) should be placed on the list.

On the bottom of the form is a section entitled "Misc. To-/Do-'s." Here you list such things as: pick up blouse from cleaners, make appointment for manicure, hire babysitter, borrow Marcia's card table, pick up game prizes, order flowers, etc.

Now, post the party planner in a convenient spot or keep it in your planning notebook. Whenever a thought strikes, jot it down on your planner so it won't be forgotten and come back to haunt you later on.

Ten days to two weeks before the get-together, invite your guests in writing or just give them a call. During hectic holiday seasons, three to four weeks notice is better.

Whether the invitation is oral or written, be sure to include the address and directions to your home (or the party location), type of party, dress, time, and date. It's best not to ask for regrets only, because you'll just worry that someone forgot to call—and they might. Stick to R.S.V.P.

Remember, too, the spur-of-the-moment parties are often the most fun of all. But even these require some fore-thought.

Other things to do ten to fourteen days before: fill out party planner; hire babysitter and/or other help; order any specialties—flowers, deli, bakery, butcher, liquor, decorations; reserve anything you need to rent or borrow (chairs, tables, chafing dishes, snack sets, etc.); polish silver and wash seldom-used glassware and china.

CULINARY ARTS

Whether your party is a spur-of-the-moment fling or a seriously premeditated affair, you need to take special precautions when planning your menu—especially when time is of the essence.

I have a good friend who is a professional caterer. She has four basic menu plans she normally offers (though she will fill special requests). I think that's a great policy to incorporate at home, too.

With standard menus you become very proficient at making the dishes; you know the approximate cost (in terms of time and money), you know what can be made ahead, and since they're tried and true, you have a pretty good idea that the guests will enjoy the entrees.

You'll notice at the end of the chart there's a ten-minute time cushion for last-minute checks. Finish tidying up the kitchen. If you've been cleaning as you go this won't be much of a job. Double check the table and set out anything that will not be affected by room temperature for ten to twenty minutes or so. Recheck your party planner to make sure you have set out all the food. More than once I've discovered a wonderful (but forgotten) salad when I'm putting things away after dinner. And finally, check the bathrooms to be sure the towels are still fresh and to wipe up any drips.

AROUND THE HOUSE LIKE MAGIC

Unfortunately, throwing a party usually includes housecleaning, so that chore needs to be scheduled as well. But there are a few tricks I've learned from expert party-givers that keep cleaning to a minimum.

One such expert is a professional housekeeper. She says the most important places to spruce up are: mirrors, any glass (light fixtures, visible windows), and cobwebs. She maintains that sparkling glass and dust-free ceilings (especially at night) make the whole house appear clean.

Another expert takes this approach: "Forget cleaning! Oh sure, you have to vacuum and straighten things up a bit and have at least one bathroom livable, but turn off the lights and use a lot of candles. Then, save your cleaning for after the party. More than likely, it'll need it!" She's right. Candles mask a lot of dust, fingerprints, and waterspots. Besides, everyone looks much better in candlelight.

I have a friend who is a wonderful entertainer and she thoroughly cleans only the rooms where guests will likely be. All other rooms are darkened and their doors closed. Her house is so attractive, people frequently ask her to show them every room. (That's what scares the rest of us!) But, my friend is a pro. She just laughs and says, "Are you kidding? I wouldn't let you into those awful rooms if you had a note from St. Peter!"

Another effective way to get the most from a cleaning session is to have two parties back to back. You not only clean once and celebrate twice, you can double up on food preparation, decorations, equipment, etc., and save all the get ready and cleanup of two separate affairs.

Some of you might have been swayed by a few of the above ideas. But, if you're like me, you're going to fear that someone will snag her pantyhose and snoop around in the bathroom for a bottle of clear nail polish to stop the run. Or (and it never fails) one of the kids will scamper into the living room and ask one of the guests if she'd like to see her bedroom. Or, someone will comment on your lovely antique buffet while innocently opening one of the doors vhich reveal your single sock collection, extra notebook paper, three unfinished projects, a shredded catnip mouse, and a sweat shirt you shoved in there when the doorbell rang.

So, if you must clean, do down-under stuff (straightening drawers, closets, vacuuming under furniture, washing windows, dusting Levolors, days before the party and maintain your efforts until party time. Then, when you have a little free time on party day, dust and vacuum where needed, clean bathrooms, check flowers, pillows, candles, etc. and other last minute, light jobs.

If you've allowed a large enough time cushion on your time plan you should have thirty to sixty minutes of relaxed time before the guests arrive. Any white area on your timetable is free time.

FOLLOW-UP AND FILE

After the guests go home, or the next day, spend a few minutes to complete the follow-up form. Actually, you can start filling out this form as soon as you decide to have a party. Use it in conjunction with the party planner, filling in the date, place, theme or occasion, decorations, guests, etc. After the party, fill in the remainder of the form.

Under "comments," record any impressions you had about the success of the party. What would you do differently? What seemed to work really well? Here is where you might say: "No one commented on the cranberry salad and there was a lot left over."

Or, "Everyone loved the cheese roll."

The entertainment section is where you jot down what games you played (and the response) or if you used professional entertainment. Note who, what, and cost.

Guest information is especially helpful when planning future events. I record things like this. Roberta doesn't like sweet and sour. Rick loves cherry pie. Dan and Steve don't get along too well. Ann's favorite flavor is burnt almond fudge. Yvonne admired my handmade doilies.

Here's how I put this information to good use. We keep our name and address list in a Rolodex file instead of an address book. With each person listed on a separate card, there's plenty of room to jot down useful information. Besides, it's easier to keep names in alphabetical order when they're individually organized instead of listed.

Anyway, on the back of Roberta's card, let's say, I either make a note about the sweet/sour or write the date of the party, which will refer me to the entertainment file. Then I staple the party planner, the follow-up sheet, and the timetable (if I used one) together and put them chronologically in the entertainment file. The next time I invite Roberta to a party, I check the back of her card and it leads me to the party planner that refers to her.

These notes not only help me to be a more thoughtful hostess, but when Yvonne's birthday comes up, she'll be awfully surprised when she receives a pretty lace doily.

I keep track of a lot of things: names of children, upcoming trips or other special events, hospital stays, favorite colors or flowers—anything that someday might help me say, "I care about you."

In addition, the party planner and follow-up sheets help to plan future parties. In the future you can invite different people and have the exact party all over again. Most of the preliminary planning will already be done.

Even though you're not a professional caterer it's important to develop a few specialties. Choose recipes that can be made a day ahead (or way ahead and frozen), so you won't have to do a lot of cooking on the day of the party. When planning your menu, choose something you've made before so you won't be surprised by a last-minute flop.

Over the years I've collected some great party recipes I can serve with confidence. They're always met with rave reviews and requests for the recipes. (As a matter of fact, when no one asks for

Escape from the Kitchen

FOLLOW-UP

PARTY DATE: ⸺⸺⸺⸺⸺⸺⸺⸺⸺⸺⸺⸺⸺

PLACE: ⸺⸺⸺⸺⸺⸺⸺⸺⸺⸺⸺⸺⸺⸺

SPECIAL OCCASION OR THEME: ⸺⸺⸺⸺⸺⸺

DECORATIONS: ⸺⸺⸺⸺⸺⸺⸺⸺⸺⸺⸺⸺

⸺⸺⸺⸺⸺⸺⸺⸺⸺⸺⸺⸺⸺⸺⸺⸺⸺⸺

Guests:

WHAT I WORE: ⸺⸺⸺⸺⸺⸺⸺⸺⸺⸺⸺

Hired help: Who, what for, cost, comments:

ENOUGH FOOD: ⸺⸺⸺ *ENOUGH/PROPER EQUIPMENT?* ⸺⸺

ENTERTAINMENT: ⸺⸺⸺⸺⸺⸺⸺⸺⸺⸺

⸺⸺⸺⸺⸺⸺⸺⸺⸺⸺⸺⸺⸺⸺⸺⸺⸺⸺

⸺⸺⸺⸺⸺⸺⸺⸺⸺⸺⸺⸺⸺⸺⸺⸺⸺⸺

⸺⸺⸺⸺⸺⸺⸺⸺⸺⸺⸺⸺⸺⸺⸺⸺⸺⸺

Comments:

Guest Information:

the recipe, I feel just awful!) So, if you don't currently have any specialties, pore over some cookbooks and try lots of new ideas. Pretty soon you'll hit upon a few good recipes you can always rely on.

Plan your main course first and additional courses around that. Keep all the food simple and complementary. Choose food that waits well in case guests arrive late. Don't be afraid to serve commercially prepared foods in addition to those that are homemade. Keep in mind, too, any guest preferences you're aware of (Emily is a vegetarian, Jean is allergic to nuts, Jim is on a diet).

Does the season or occasion suggest a menu? International fare is perfect for a bon voyage party; football season is a good "kick-off" for a picnic—tailgate style; early Spring is a nice time for a brunch, since it gives you a chance to make good the social obligations you've been collecting all winter.

How about asking guests to furnish part of the meal? Specify appetizer, dessert, salad, rolls, etc. Today, with everyone's busy time schedules, no one seems to mind taking over some of the food assignments.

Another way to get out from under food preparation time is to make fixing dinner part of the entertainment. This works especially well when there are not too many guests. Have one guest chop, another fry, another toss a salad, and so on. Or, plan a meal (such as a stir-fry or fondue) that can be prepared right at the table. Buffets where you make your own sundaes, design an omelet, or assemble a Hero are tasty, fun, and easy on the hostess.

Pick up food from a favorite restaurant; my favorites are Chinese or Mexican food because they reheat quickly. The deli is a great source for cheeses, salads, luncheon meats, etc. They also fix nice platters that save you hours of chopping, slicing, coring, and so on. Top these off with a luscious dessert (homemade or purchased), and you've got a no-hassle winner.

One thing we do occasionally is to have everyone meet at our house for appetizers, then we choose a restaurant for dinner. Then it's back to our house for dessert and a game of Trivial Pursuit.

Before or after any event (ballet, theater, sporting event, etc.) is an ideal time for a get-together. This type of entertaining lends itself well to appetizers or dessert service only—a real time saver. Some of my favorite parties, by the way, are ones where only appetizers and desserts are served.

MANAGING
THE BIG MEAL

Now, more than ever before, it's important to follow the rules for general maintenance you read earlier in the book. Fill the sink or a dishpan with hot, sudsy water. Spread a sheet of freezer wrap or newspaper on the kitchen counter. Set out a handy trash container near your working center. This clean-as-you-go process gets you out of the kitchen faster than any other single thing you do, especially when you're working on a big meal.

The following is a time plan for scheduling big meals so everything is ready at the same time. The time plan also helps you serve hot foods hot and cold foods cold and if it's done correctly, the kitchen will be presentable, too.

These time plans are extremely helpful when you're serving a multicourse meal and they're good practice for beginning cooks who want to polish their culinary skills. With experience, everyday meals do not require the precision of a written timetable, but even though I have years of cooking experience under my belt (literally and figuratively) I always use a time plan for big and important meals.

Here's what you do. First, list your menu and all nonfood jobs on your party planner. Also decide what can be done a day or more ahead, and schedule it on your calendar or note it on the party planner.

Here are some good jobs to do ahead: Set the table, crisp the fresh vegetables and salad greens, arrange relish trays, make stuffing (but don't stuff poultry until just before cooking), butter French bread and wrap in foil, whip topping, make dips and salad dressings, measure water and salt for cooking frozen vegetables, potatoes, rice, etc., set salads, make rolls and dessert. Serving tables and dishes can be set out a few days before the party if you're pressed for time.

To keep made-ahead sandwiches fresh, place a damp towel in the bottom of a shallow pan. The edges of the towel should hang over the sides of the pan. Place waxed paper over the damp cloth and stack sandwiches in the pan, putting waxed paper between each layer of sandwiches. After placing a final layer of waxed paper on the top of the sandwiches, fold the towel over them.

Next, what food will require the longest preparation time. Let's say your menu plans call for homemade crescent rolls which you estimate will take 2½ hours. If you're serving dinner at 7:30, then you must start the rolls no later than 5:00, right? Better yet, start them at 4:30. It's always smart to allow yourself a little extra time so you'll have a cushion for cleaning as you go and for any unplanned interruptions.

Now, draw up a columnar chart as illustrated on page 164. Allow one column for every dish in your menu plan. Any last-minute nonfood jobs should also be recorded, i.e., light the candles, spot check the house, turn on the stereo, threaten the kids one last time. Then after you've blocked off the time segments needed for each entree, read the chart from left to right and downward. That way you start everything at the right time and hopefully finish at the same time.

Here's an example. In the crescent roll column, darken the spaces between 4:30 and 4:50. Those twenty minutes will be used to mix and knead the dough. The dough will rise between 4:50 and 5:40 and will not require any attention, so leave those spaces blank. From 5:40 to 5:50 the dough will be rolled, cut, and set to rise again. Darken the 5:40 to 5:50 area. The rolls will need no further tending until 7:00, when you bake them. Darken 7:00 to 7:20.

TIPS FOR A HEARTY PARTY

- After cleaning the house for the last time before the party, if you need to feed the kids, cut out the front of a big cardboard box and put it on the floor in front of the TV. Serve the kids right in the carton. It keeps crumbs off the floor and fascinates the kids. (Or keep them occupied in the box working on a craft.)

- A babysitter can take the children out for hamburgers and a movie and bring them home and put them to bed. Or, have the sitter babysit in the children's rooms.

- When fixing the refreshments, pack a small box or bag of goodies for each child and send it with them when they go to their rooms (or into the far reaches to watch a video).

- Put a signal on your house so guests will be able to spot it more easily. (Tie a bow around your mailbox, display a colorful banner, paint a message on poster board, using luminous paint.)

Dish	Stroganoff Mix, Cook	Wild Rice Prep & Cook	Peas & Onions Cook	Salad— Do-Ahead	Crescent Rolls	Choc. Chip Cake—Do Ahead	Beverage Mix—Pour	Set Table	Final Clean-up Check
7:30	▓	▓	▓						▓
7:20	▓	▓	▓		▓		▓		▓
7:10	▓	▓	▓		▓		▓		▓
7:00	▓	▓							▓
6:50	▓								
6:40	▓								
6:30	▓								
6:20								▓	
6:10								▓	
6:00								▓	
5:50					▓				
5:40									
5:30									
5:20									
5:10									
5:00									
4:50					▓				
4:40									

- When using placecards at a sit-down dinner, be sure to write the guests' names on both sides of the card. That way if the visitors are not well acquainted, they'll know to whom they are speaking during dinner.

- If you're expecting a big crowd and you have only a small house, serve food in different rooms. Set up tables and chairs anywhere there's available space or serve the appetizers in the living room, salads in the kitchen, main dishes in the den, etc. This keeps the crowd moving and mingling—yet no one area will be overly congested.

- Use an ice bucket for serving food. Because it's insulated it keeps things either hot or cold.

- Dried fruits arranged on a platter are great appetizers. They require no preparation, they're delicious, and are ready and waiting for guests who arrive at any time.

- When serving sandwiches, cut them in different ways to serve as a code. (Diagonally cut sandwiches have mayonnaise, horizontally cut have mustard.)

- Use your automatic coffeemaker to steep cider, cinnamon sticks, cloves, and allspice. (The spices go in the coffee basket.) Brew as usual.

- For a one-of-a-kind tablecloth, use a white sheet and let your guest sign it, using a permanent laundry marker. Use the same cloth at all your parties, so the guest list keeps growing.

- A bread and butter party is easy and inexpensive, not to mention good tasting. Serve a wide assortment of breads and flavored butters. If you want to, add an array of cheese, cold meat, raw vegetables, and fruits.

- Have a snack-luck party. Everyone brings their favorite snack. You provide the beverages. Or, have a simple buffet where you serve mugs of soup, salads, rolls, and dessert.

- Start up a lending co-op with your close friends. Everyone lists the things they've got plenty of and would be willing to share (snack sets, folding chairs, card tables, chafing dishes). Type up a list and circulate it among the members of the group. This works very well for people who live in tight quarters.

- Next time you have a bridal shower, tell everyone to bring some household goods they no longer use or want (in addition to a new gift). It's a great way to get rid of things.

- Pack leftovers in decorated doggie bags and give to your friends when they leave the party. (Great for diet-conscious hosts and hostesses.)

If you'd like to feel like a guest at your own party try some of these ideas. Even if you quail at the thought of having a party, even if your days are as crowded as Joan Collins' closet, even if your house is more like a hovel, there's a party you can give with a flourish.

Once you've absorbed this bit of education, you can move on to your entertaining doctorate. Let the ideas in this chapter serve as a springboard for your own ingenuity and you'll discover that entertaining is an enjoyable part of life—for guests and hosts alike.

chapter 11

'TWAS THE BLIGHT BEFORE CHRISTMAS

Someday I'd like to meet Mrs. Clement Clark Moore. Her husband, you recall, wrote: " 'Twas the night before Christmas when all through the house, not a creature was stirring, not even a mouse."

Imagine, not a creature stirring on Christmas Eve! Mrs. Moore, with her donned kerchief and settled brains (another amazing Christmas Eve feat), was not exactly dressed for success, yet somehow she managed to hang the stockings with care by the chimney, nestle her children all snug in their beds, and still have time for a long winter's nap! Amazing.

One year the Christmas season was so frantic around our house, I wrote myself a letter (after the fact) outlining the gory details. Here are a few highlights:

Dec. 12: Searched rain gutter for Christmas tree lights. Still there, but not in good shape after a year of outdoor storage.

Dec. 14: Jeffrey wrote a letter to Santa Claus saying, "It isn't fair to leave presents for only good kids."

Dec. 17: Kids made and decorated sugar cookies to give to their friends. Since we had only one rolling pin, it seemed natural that any dough needing to be flattened be sat upon. Flour stuck like hard paste to the counters, table, and floor. Colored sprinkles and a

168

Escape from the Kitchen

rainbow of Christmas-colored icings dribbled down chair, table, and human legs, only to dry as if caught in a moment of suspended animation. With the aid of a putty knife, two aspirin, and a lot of "Bah-Humbugs," the kitchen was temporarily put back in order.

Dec. 18: Delivered sugar cookies to kids' friends after visiting the convalescent center, rehearsing for the Christmas play, taking a case of canned goods to the sub-for-Santa site; but before the Jr. High choir concert, the office party, and the trip downtown to see the lights.

Dec. 20: Spent most of the day doing Christmas cards.

Dec. 21: Christmas baking for my friends.

Dec. 22: Christmas baking for my friends. Hated every minute of this baking session. Had more important things to do, but a strong sense of obligation kept me going. Couldn't just say, "Thanks," when friends shoved baskets and tins full of homemade goodies into my arms. Hated cookies, nutbreads, and candy. Hated friends.

Dec. 23: Delivered baked goods to friends. Went to Erma's. She asked if I'd just made the cookies. Said, "Yes." Asked how she knew. Erma pointed to the two flour handprints on my backside (which I always find more convenient than a hand towel). Hated Erma. Later that night turned Christmas carolers away empty handed. All the baked treats had been given away. Didn't make any for our family.

Dec. 24: Hunched over unwrapped presents with hands on knees as though losing a bout with indigestion. Used all the newspapers and comics. Wrapped rest of presents in brown paper bags. Smeared a lot of camouflage stick under my eyes.

Many times during the next year I reread my letter, using it as motivation to organize and enjoy future holidays. The trick worked!

Whether you want to celebrate a child's grand slam home run, or capture the spirit of the holidays, keep reading. Here's how I went from an also-ran to in-the-running. If you pay close attention, you'll not only pick up a lot of escape-from-the-kitchen ideas, you'll be able to enjoy any celebration with more gusto!

PLAN, PLAN, PLAN

Unplanned expenditures of time will do more to ruin things than trees on a baseball field. Take a few minutes early in the season and begin planning. I begin my serious holiday planning in the summer. However, more casual planning could begin as late as September or October. Waiting until Thanksgiving, though, is too late. List gifts to make, gifts to buy, cards purchased and addressed, baking, mailing gifts and cards, making decorations, buying the tree, decorating the house—whatever you can think of.

Write these plans down. When you have a tangible list to look at you can use your physical senses as well as your mental processes. It's impossible to organize, prioritize, and pare down a mental note. So, write down everything you can think of that needs to be done—even if you know you won't be able to do it all.

Talk to school teachers early in the school year to find out about school holiday activities. Will there be after-school rehearsals, evening performances, special costumes required, or anything else you can plan for?

If you're a serious holiday celebrate-er, set aside a holiday section in your planning notebook where you record gift ideas, plans for the upcoming event, gift and card lists, and so forth. That way you can cash in on sales all year long and eliminate some of the last-minute frenzy. Also, include in this section the layouts of your favorite department stores:

Nelson's Dept. Store: First Floor:cosmetics, shoes, purses, accessories, stationery, books

Second Floor:clothing—men, women, children

Call your chamber of commerce and ask what your town has planned for the holidays. Schedule those chosen activities on your calendar so you can plan ahead and work around them.

Whenever possible, use the layaway services of a large department store. If you purchase all (or a majority) of your gifts in one store, you'll have your shopping done in a few hours; and using layaway means you don't need cash-in-hand (though a deposit is usually required). Laying things away forces you to plan ahead so you can shop before the crowds frazzle your nerves and limit your selection. Also, for gifts going out of town, many stores will send them for you. We frequently buy all our gifts in a local department store. Everything is put on layaway in late October. In December, we pick up the gifts and the store wraps them for free!

Escape from the Kitchen

Meal planning will save hours of time. Even if you never do it, do it now, at least. Select simple meals so you can serve hot, nourishing food during the hectic weeks coming up. Start dinner and bake after breakfast so you can have one cleanup. From Halloween until Christmas, bake and freeze varieties of cookies so you can have a large assortment ready without much hassle.

Now that you have some plans and ideas scribbled down, look over the list and check off only those things you feel are especially important, and schedule them in your calendar. Roughly prioritize the rest of the list and schedule as many things as you can *realistically* handle. One of the best ways to save time and escape from the kitchen is to take the emphasis off food—particularly as gifts. (Some specific ideas follow.)

Cut back as much as possible. Everyone will enjoy the season much more if you're not under so much pressure.

Must you have a *Christmas* party? Why not schedule a party for some other time of the year? Or have a holiday get-together between Christmas and New Year's? There's sometimes a lull in people's schedule during that week.

Instead of sending a newsy Christmas letter, why not do it on Valentine's Day? One of my friends does this every year and the results have been surprising. She used to send the letter at Christmas but decided it just added to her usual holiday frustrations. So, one year she typed up her letter and mailed it to close friends and relatives on Valentine's Day. It was such a hit with everyone (because everyone else had more time to enjoy it), she's continued the practice.

Another friend enjoyed homemade food gifts but, as always, time was too hard to come by after Thanksgiving. Now she delivers her gifts just before Thanksgiving with a lovely card expressing her gratitude for good friends and wishing them a happy holiday season. Isn't that a great idea! It accomplishes the purpose of the holiday season; it's more thoughful (less obligatory), less hurried, and probably more appreciated by the receiver.

A neighborhood basket is a wonderful time saver. Here's how it worked in one neighborhood we lived in. One family filled a basket with special treats and passed the basket on to the family next door. The basket was refilled and passed along from house to house. It was a good way to say, "Happy Holidays," to each other without fixing individual gifts.

Here's something I just started doing and I think it's going to be a winner. I love homemade crafts, and like to share them with friends and especially my family. But handwork is so time-consuming (and my family is so large) it seemed impossible to whip something up for everyone.

Enter the Christmas Idea Box. As soon as Christmas is over I start making simple little projects (decorations, ornaments, or nonseasonal house decorations, etc.). These are usually portable and I never walk out of the house without something to do. So, most of the crafts are assembled during waiting or transportation time, during ballgames, or while TV watching.

Then in July or early August I assemble the idea boxes, putting a few of the finished projects in each (along with the instructions). I write a letter to each recipient saying that I'm sending their gifts early enough so they can, in turn, make some for their friends and relatives. You see, it really is Christmas in July.

This has been so much fun. All year long I feel the warm spirit of giving; yet, I'm actually spending less time than I was before. Because I've planned early and used up snatches of time I would have otherwise wasted, my holidays are much less stressful. I have more time for sleigh rides, snowball fights, reading by the fire, and enjoying (rather than begrudging) the season.

Holidays can be stressful for children, too. The anticipation and excitement of the season sometimes turns even the most docile child into a cross between Charo and Mr. T. Some psychologists recommend alleviating some of the tension by giving the child a few token or trinket gifts occasionally before Christmas.

So, I made an advent calendar with twenty-four pockets in it. Inside each pocket I place a piece of paper on which is written the location of a hidden treat. These daily presents are simple things like: a pencil, comb, gum, cereal box trinkets (I collect and save them during the year), a holiday cookie, balloons, stickers, and the like. This has proven to be one of our favorite traditions and has helped the kids cope with the anxiety and me to experience peace on earth and goodwill towards children.

GIFT IDEAS TO HELP YOU ESCAPE

Once again, take the emphasis off food gifts—especially the "homemade, slave away for hours" kind—if you want to escape from your kitchen.

Escape from the Kitchen

Here are some gift ideas for and from the kitchen that take little time, but they're thoughtful, considerate, and a refreshing change from traditional holiday treats.

One year we received one cookie and candy tray after another, and naturally we gratefully gobbled down every last piece. But by the time Christmas finally arrived we were so sick of sweets we could hardly face another bon bon or piece of toffee. That's when I decided to start giving fruit instead of candy, cakes, and cookies. (The truth is, I stopped giving candy because, as a candy maker, I make a great bricklayer. As my kids always say after I make fudge, "This tastes great, Mom. It's *hard*, but it's good!"

During the year I collect inexpensive baskets and then in early December I fill them with fruit: oranges, apples, grapefruit, pineapple, kiwi, etc., whatever is plentiful. Wrapped in cellophane (clear or colored) and topped with a bow, these fruit baskets are well received by everyone and more appreciated now that everyone seems increasingly health and diet conscious. In one hour (including shopping time) I can have a counter full of gift baskets ready. A counter full of cookies would have taken most of one day.

In addition to the common sources, thrift stores, garage sales, and flea markets are wonderful places to find inexpensive, unusual, or one-of-a-kind containers in which to pack your gift, be it homemade or purchased food, or a useful tool.

Remember, your food goodies do not have to be homemade to be appreciated. If you're uncomfortable with that, try putting a purchased food treat in an unusual or practical container. For some reason, it restores your feeling of pride.

Some good containers to look for: bottles, baskets, wooden bowls, wineglasses, brontainers in which to pack your gift, be it homemade or purchased food, or a useful tool.

Remember, your food goodies do not have to be homemade to be appreciated. If you're uncomfortable with that, try putting a purchased food treat in an unusual or practical container. For some reason, it restores your feeling of pride.

Some good containers to look for: bottles, baskets, wooden bowls, wineglasses, brandy snifters, beakers, crocks, pitchers (small and large), jugs, bowls, mugs, canisters, trays, beanpots, glazed pottery casseroles, scoops, dessert molds, souffle dishes, mixing bowls, pans (all types), oven mitts, ice buckets, cookie tins, flour sifters, nut choppers, muffin pans, porcelain teacups, and salt and pepper shakers. (The teacups and shakers are especially nice for collectors.)

- Give fresh herbs growing in tiny clay pots. Or, present dried herbs in ceramic canisters, small decorative tins, or any pretty container.

- Pour seasoned oil, vinegar, or salad dressings into cruets or one-of-a-kind bottles. Top with a cork and tie a pretty ribbon around each neck.

- Give some seasoned salt in a new shaker or how about giving a peppermill and a can of peppercorns? Put hot cocoa mix in a large colorful mug or other creative container.

- Wrap up a package of wooden skewers with a gift of olives or pickles.

- Heap colorful produce (tomatoes, peppers, fruit) into a brass, graniteware, or other decorative colander.

- Coverall aprons are always nice to receive. If you like, tuck a few kitchen tools or food treats inside the apron pockets.

- For the omelet connoisseur, give a flexible spatula, herbs, and a favorite omelet recipe. Or give the recipe for cherries jubilee with a half-gallon of vanilla ice cream. Fancy pasta is the perfect accompaniment to your minestrone recipe. For a main dish, put the directions and a key ingredient in a new casserole dish.

- Give a favorite recipe as a gift and include one of the ingredients (ginger snaps with a sauerbraten recipe, walnuts for sugared walnuts, cinnamon sticks with a mulled cider recipe). Put a box of gelatin inside a copper mold and include the recipe for a delicious set salad or dessert. Pour cornmeal into a novel container, add a recipe for corn bread and tie on a wooden spoon.

- Collect a few favorite recipes from the recipient's friends and relatives and give her the collection in a card file or notebook. (Be sure to include the name of the donor on each recipe.) Or, fill a notebook or card file with your own favorite recipes.

- Fill a tote bag with small kitchen gadgets (peeler, apple corer, bottle stoppers, tongs, melon baller, skewers, measuring spoons, spatulas, etc.). Tie something to a wire whisk, ladle, or large wooden spoon.

- Cents-off coupons for products your friend uses are a very practical gift idea. Fill a basket with canned goods or cleaning supplies and tuck the coupons inside.

- If you want to spend hours putting faces on gingerbread men, that's fine. But, if time is working against you, these are nice and easy foods to give: berries, fruits, jams, jellies, honey, cheese spreads, flavored butters, salted or spiced nuts, nuts in the shell, popcorn, popcorn balls, caramel corn, candy, dried fruit, citron, purchased bakery products, and so on.

- Also, think about things everyone always needs and frequently runs out of: paper towels, dish cloths and towels, candles (tie a bunch of tapers together with a bright ribbon), bag of charcoal, stamps, recipe cards, batteries, glasses, ice-cream dishes, fireplace logs, paper plates and cups, plastic tableware, immersion coil, ice-cream scoop (box it up and include some Baskin-Robbins coupons), hand lotion, memo pads (Post It notes are great), herb seeds, or gift certificates. Find some odd saucers and fit each with a fat candle in white or harmonize with the saucer's color, etc.

- Sew up some simple cloth pouches and fill with potpourri, bouquet garni, herbs, candy, etc.

- Or, how about a new cookbook? Write an inscription on the inside cover and put a star by each of your favorite recipes. A serious cook would likely appreciate a subscription to *Gourmet* magazine (or something similar).

- One year my sister Judy gave us a big popcorn bucket. She purchased a large metal bucket, spray-painted the outside and attached several decals. She also got eight tin cups and decorated them to match. (All in all, this was a thirty minute job.) To finish the gift, she included a 2-lb. bag of unpopped popcorn. That bucket served us faithfully for many years. It was practical, cute, and not time-costly.

- Give a gift of candy in an apothecary jar, ice-cube tray, desk organizer, or kitchen drawer divider.

- A brandy snifter displays and contains a selection of hard candies, spiced nuts, jelly beans, or whatever.

- Canisters for flour and sugar are nice for cookies, nuts, popcorn, caramel corn, crackers, or pretzels.

- Deep, large scoops are creative containers for candies, gourmet popcorn (unpopped), doughnut holes, jelly beans, or whatever. Fill, and cover with plastic wrap, then add a festive bow.

- Fill up a toy with cookies and/or candy, etc. Good choices are: plastic boats and dump trucks, lunch boxes, bicycle baskets, sandpails, or any toy with a hollow space large enough to accommodate the treat.

- Fill different-sized Mason jars with jelly beans, wrap the lids with colorful calico, and tie with yarn or ribbon. Set the bottles on tables, mantles, windowsills, etc., to use as party decorations. When your guests go home, give each one a jar of the jelly beans.

- Hang gingerbread men from houseplants, house trees, mantles, etc., and give to carolers and other guests.

- Give a cake mix wrapped in a new cake pan. Include a box or can of frosting and a decorating tool.

- Give a purchased or homemade cake on a new baking pan. Put cookies on a shiny new cookie sheet or in an ice bucket.

- Steam a pudding or bake a bundt cake in a new pan and give it as a present.

- Fill a punch bowl, salad bowl, colander, or bread box with doughnuts, sweet rolls, bread, or popcorn.

- Put a colorful kitchen hand towel in a basket and fill with muffins, bagels, cookies, etc.

- Present bread on a cutting board. Pack cheese spread, flavored butters, or canape spreads in a pate mold, ramekin, crock, or ceramic jar, and attach a spreader.

- Wrap a gift of bread (homemade or bakery) in a festive dish towel (or one that matches the recipient's kitchen decor) and tie with ribbon or yarn.

- A person who lives alone might enjoy a selection of frozen, single-serving portions of dinners cooked for your own family. Top it off with a beverage, rolls, and dessert portions.

- Take some lunch bags or decorative paper tote bags to the printer and have your message transferred onto them. (Treats from Trixie's Kitchen.) Or, have them printed with your friend's name and give her the whole stack! They're cute and creative as gift containers. (Another idea is to have a large rubber stamp printed and make your own.)

- Instead of tying a bow on top of your gift, why not attach a Chore Girl or plastic scrubber.

- To inexpensively package any homemade treat, save TV dinner trays and fill with an assortment of things. Styrofoam meat trays are available at any butcher department for just a few cents each. They, too, are handy for containing your homemade foods.

The whole idea is to think creatively. You'll be amazed to discover how much time you can save just by thinking. Don't be afraid to do something different. It's much more fun for you and a pleasant surprise for the receivers.!

SPECIAL WAYS FOR SPECIAL DAYS

- For a nice hostess gift, bring your favorite appetizer. It will definitely be appreciated!

- Bringing punch to a party? Pour a few inches into a milk carton and freeze. Refrigerate the rest. When it's time to go, pour the cold punch over the frozen. The solid layer will keep the beverage cold and won't dilute the mixture.

- Nursing homes and hospitals are swamped with generous offers during holiday seasons (especially Easter, Thanksgiving, and Christmas). Why not schedule your organization's visit and gifts for another time during the year? Your attention may be more appreciated then and everyone in your group won't be quite as busy.

- Welcome new neighbors with a pounding party. Everyone brings a pound of a staple food (flour, sugar, rice, etc.). On move-in day, treat the new family to a casserole or dessert, and don't forget the paper plates, cups, and plastic forks.

- Buy a few sets of soaps, jams, candles, or herbal teas. Take them apart and use as token gifts for unexpected guests or as an "extra touch" for a prepared gift.

- Send a hostess gift when your child sleeps or eats at a friend's house—a bottle of juice, a box of cookies, a bag of Popsicles. It's a nice way to begin teaching your child about gratitude.

- For a child whose birthday comes in the dead of winter (especially close to Christmas) how about a half-birthday party? One year my sister decided to have one for her son, whose birthday is December 24. For invitations, she made and frosted a batch of cupcakes and divided each one in half, cutting from top to bottom. Then she used extra frosting to mount each cupcake to small pieces of poster board on which was printed the half-birthday invitation. Each edible invitation was then hand-delivered. For the first time Michael had a summer birthday and enjoyed warm weather events. (It's a much better time of year to get a new bike, too.)

- Make edible placecards by writing (with a tube of icing) the child's name on a sugar cookie.

- For a birthday party activity, have each child decorate his own birthday cake. Bake one for each child using a small round cake pan from a play set. Be sure it's ovenproof, though, before you use it.

- For any special occasion, give the children pieces of felt to be used as placemats. Let the kids decorate them with felt cut outs, stickers, paint, or whatever.

- For an easy special touch, mold gelatin in clean plastic toys (horse head shovel, cars, castles, clay molds, etc.).

- Fill ice-cream cones with tuna, egg, chicken salad, cottage cheese, or yogurt.

- Plan a picnic for the kids. All invitees bring their own lunch. You provide the blankets, punch, and dessert.

- On days when the kids are baking (as long as you're going to have a mess anyway) why not invite one of their friends? Choose someone who needs cheering up (such as a child whose parents are divorcing) or a child new to the neighborhood. One year we invited a Japanese boy who had just arrived in the United States and couldn't speak English. Old friends are fine, too, but it's nice to occasionally include a child who just needs a friend.

- When making cookies for Easter, cut egg-shaped dough, sprinkle with colored sugar, and bake. They come out speckled—just like *real* bird eggs.

- Use candy canes as swizzle sticks in eggnog.

- For a special (no extra time) touch at dinner, fill a brandy snifter with crisp, raw vegetables. Sprinkle crushed ice on top.

- One evening a month, serve a foreign specialty and set the table accordingly.

- When serving the family beef stew, chili, a one-dish casserole, or other "cowboy grub," use bandannas as napkins, pie pans for dishes, and small Mason jars for glasses.

- Make quick centerpieces with what you already have on hand: shiny apples look great piled in a bowl, or core them and use for candle holders. Drop limes, cherry tomatoes, nuts, or pinecones in a glass jar or airy woven basket.

- If you can't afford to take the whole family out for dinner but want to enjoy a meal out once in a while, eat breakfast out instead. Breakfast meals are cheaper (and usually faster).

- For a "nice touch" breakfast, why not provide room service to the children or your spouse. A continental breakfast of juice, sweet rolls, and/or toast, and hot chocolate is easy, yet it conveys your special thoughts.

This chapter has more ideas than the patent office, so you're left with no excuses. This year, before you get involved in an all-night wrapping session, stop for a moment. Promise yourself that once and for all you will have peace on earth at your house. Plan well, prepare early, and on Christmas Eve not a creature will stir.

chapter 12

BY DESIGN

Is there a kitchen counter revolution in your future? Are you planning guerrilla warfare with a "take no prisoners" approach, hiring a crew large enough to man the Vatican guard, and overseeing the removal of planet-size chunks from your existing kitchen? Great!

Even though it's a messy job, it can be exciting and fun from the first planning steps to the first load of dishes in your new kitchen. Everyone enjoys a new kitchen for many, many years and if it's done right, a good kitchen will appreciate the value of your home.

However, maybe you're thinking more of a "coup" than a revolution: a few cosmetic changes, a couple of added conveniences—maybe things Cousin Egbert could do on Saturday afternoons.

No matter your approach or what the desired result, there are some important things to consider before you begin.

PLAN FIRST

Even before you begin perusing magazines, kitchen design catalogs, and model home interiors, you need to begin thinking about your lifestyle, your desired lifestyle, and your particular needs. Knowing these things in advance will help your kitchen designer, architect, or handyman give you exactly what you want *and* need.

To get you started, here is a Lifestyle Questionnaire. Jot down the answers so you'll have something tangible to work with. Star the items that are most important to you. That way if it's impossible to get everything you want, your designer will at least know your priorities.

1. **Do you want a major overhaul or just a new face?** Are you just bored with your old kitchen or is it seriously dysfunctional?

Generally speaking, if your kitchen is newer than ten years old, a retouch is probably all you need. Unless, of course, serious structural problems are causing time or space difficulties.

Maybe new countertops, flooring, cupboard doors, or appliances would be enough to perk things up. There are many specialty shops that refinish existing cabinets, replace cupboard fronts, or install plastic laminate surfaces which can update a drab look. New fluorescent lighting does wonders for kitchen work areas.

But if you're ready for a knock-down drag-out fight, here's what to plan for.

While a major renovation is going on, the kitchen will be closed. You will need to remove and pack up everything—food, utensils, dishes, pans, etc. Pack, label, and stack cartons containing *B* and *C* type goods, leaving only the *A*'s for daily use while you "camp-out" in another room (or on the deck or patio).

Cooking can be accomplished by means of small electric appliances, charcoal grill, immersion coil, hot plate, fry pan, crock pot, camp stove, and microwave. If possible—or if necessary—move the refrigerator to the new campsite. Dishes can be washed in the bathroom, garage, or laundry area. You may also want to include some extra fast-food or restaurant meal expenses in your kitchen planning budget.

Also, the water, gas, and electricity may have to be turned off from time to time while the workmen execute their chores. If possible, get a written time estimate from your contractor (including time, date, and length of turn-off). The day before a scheduled turn-off, recheck with your contractor to make sure the schedule is still on track.

Also, a full-blown attack on the kitchen is going to raise a lot of dust that will settle in even the nether areas of the house. Cover furniture with sheets, plastic, or drop clothes. Take any necessary precautions with carpeting or flooring you want to protect.

2. **Set limits for your time and money budgets.** Decide how much you will spend on your renovations and how long you are willing to be unsettled and living in dust. Your contractor should know exactly at the outset what you're expecting from him.

For example, it would be fair to allow six weeks (maximum) to live in the dust and chaos, and maybe an additional two to three weeks you could tolerate having some of the finer details left undone. We'll talk about finding and working with a quality crew in a minute.

3. **What do you like about your existing kitchen?** Be specific. "I like the cupboards that go clear up to the ceiling. The pantry is well-located. The long narrow cupboard is perfect for the toaster."

4. **What do you dislike about your kitchen now?** "The dishwasher is too far from the sink. The dark countertops show every crumb. The floor is dull and colorless. When we're fixing dinner, everyone gets in each other's way. I'm bothered by the street noise and the blare of the TV."

Notice the number of steps you take when you're preparing something. Do you stretch or bend continually? Make a note of these annoyances. Also consider things like the placement of the telephone and nearby storage for pens and paper.

Is there a passing traffic pattern going through kitchen work areas? Can you see into the kitchen from the front door? (My pet peeve.) Is the kitchen visible when sitting in other rooms of the house? If these things bother you, write them on your gripe list.

Pay strict attention to detail here because even the tiniest problem may pose a terrible inconvenience yet might be correctable. Case in point: when you walk into our kitchen and flip on the light switch, the backyard patio light goes on. In order to illuminate the kitchen, you have to grope and stumble, feeling your way across the room until you reach the switch (which, by the way, is next to the backyard patio). It was a small oversight that has proven to be a big pain.

5. **What is your cooking style?** How many people usually cook at once? How many people are involved in cleaning up?

What kind of a cook are you? Gourmet, vegetarian, family-style? Do you do a lot of canning, dehydrating, freezing, and baking? How about cake decorating or candy making? Do you do a lot of outdoor cooking? If so, you'll need direct access to the yard. What are your most common specialties? Your kitchen designer should be aware of any *A* or *B* type activities.

Do you use any specialty tools, appliances, or other equipment? What priority (*A-B-C*) are they? Priorities of awkward-sized equipment, especially, should be made known to your kitchen planner.

How tall is the person who does most of the cooking? A 36-inch counter is standard, but can easily be adjusted up or down— varied for comfort. (Extremes in countertop height may affect the resale of your home, so you want to carefully consider this option.)

Roll-out bins are handy for vegetables.

What types of things do you keep in drawers? Or would you like to keep in drawers? Trays, bread, files, bins for flour, sugar, potatoes, and onions?

Are you concerned with appearances, or is convenience your byword? If the latter is "you," then hanging pans and utensils, open shelves, wall-mounted dish drainers, and glass cupboard doors might be suggested. However, if everything has to be picture perfect in your kitchen, you'll have to plan plenty of undercover storage spots.

Do you want cupboards that go clear to the ceiling (providing good C-type storage on the top shelf) or do you like the decorative look of a soffit? Do you want to eliminate the soffit and display collectibles on top of your cupboards?

6. **Now, list the other types of things that go on in your kitchen.** Do you mend, wash and dry clothes, read, play games, watch TV, listen to music, participate in crafts and hobbies? Do the kids use

the kitchen as a homework center? Is your kitchen a mail room, as well? Do you want these activities to go on in your new kitchen or will some be moved to another area of the house?

At this point, be realistic and honest with yourself. You may very well decide that nary a scrap of mail will ever be placed in your new kitchen. But seriously, a year from now, after the "newness" has worn off, can you see yourself actually enforcing the new rule? If not, plan for a mail center (or whatever) now so you won't be faced with the same problems presented by your old kitchen.

7. **What have you always wanted in your kitchen?** A desk, the laundry equipment, a family room, indoor barbecue, a baking center, a deep freeze, a bump-out window seat, a rocking chair, a fireplace? Go for it. Remember, right now all we're doing is planning and dreaming. Once you have a roughly written worksheet, you can prioritize, budget, and eliminate.

8. **What is your eating style?** Do you have three meals a day, sit-down family dinners, or is it "every man for himself" during the day and one sit-down meal at night? How many people (maximum) will you want to serve at a sit-down dinner? Do you like to eat in the kitchen or would you prefer a formal dining room (or both)? My favorite arrangement is a large kitchen with a snack bar for breakfast, lunch, and snacks, a table for family dinners, and a separate dining room for special occasions.

Do you entertain often? Do you prefer formal or casual entertaining? Do you like people to visit with you in the kitchen while you cook, or do you, like Greta Garbo, want to be left alone?

Pull-out base cupboard shelves look like three drawers when closed.

Escape from the Kitchen

Your plans should be firming up like ice on a pond by now. While you're going through these questions, though, think generally about any foreseen future needs. Are you just beginning your family, or is your family starting to leave the nest? Are you planning to live in this house for a while or is a move looming in the distant future? As you progress up the corporate ladder will you be called upon to entertain clients in your home? Do you want your children to bring their friends home for pizza and ice cream after the movies? Be sure to think about your lifestyle in its present *and* future tenses.

Now that you've scribbled down a few thoughts, rewrite a neat listing of your wants and don't wants. Then, make two copies—one for you and one for your kitchen planner. Check off or star the things that are most important so you won't mistakenly axe a great idea.

Be sure you've written purposes, not solutions, on your list. For example: "Need more storage for canned goods," is a purpose. "Build slant shelves for canned goods," is a solution. Listing the purpose will enable you to consider many options, allowing you to choose more objectively the *best* solution.

Slant shelves make it easier to rotate your food supply.

NEVER TRUST A GUY NAMED CHAINSAW

Now that you know where you're going with your kitchen, it's time to find an expert.

An expert, they say, is anyone who lives fifty miles away and has a set of 35mm slides. Since your kitchen is a major investment in the value of your home, it's important to find someone with better credentials than home movies. Just because a guy has the words REMODELING painted on the side of his pick-up truck doesn't necessarily mean that you should turn over your kitchen to him.

What you're looking for is a professional who has a record of experience in the kitchen field. It is not out of line to find out how long the contractor in question has been doing business or to ask for referrals. I would be leary of anyone who doesn't have a showroom or an address listing in the phone book.

Find someone who is a designer and space planner, particularly if you're doing an in-depth renovation. The American Institute of Kitchen Dealers designates accredited kitchen representatives by the initials CKD (Certified Kitchen Dealers). They have passed exacting, qualifying tests to receive this accreditation. So, if it's possible, choose a CKD.

Since remodeling is difficult at best, choose a designer who is easy for you to work with. If you have obvious personality conflicts before the project begins, imagine how problems will balloon midstream. If your kitchen planner is very assertive, for example, you may well end up with a kitchen the way *she* wants it instead of the way *you* want it. So, choose someone you feel comfortable with and can talk to easily.

Visit showrooms and get a general idea of prices, craftsmanship, and quality grades. Talk to the salesmen and designers. With the knowledge you now have about kitchen efficiency you'll be able to discern which designers really know their stuff.

Once you've made your choice, the kitchen planner will visit your home, look over your kitchen, and take his own measurements. A truly careful professional will never accept your measurements, no matter how intelligent you may be. So don't be offended.

Once he's sized up the situation, give him a copy of your Lifestyle Questionnaire. Also, he might like to have a copy of your personalized centers' lists that show what you store in each of your work centers.

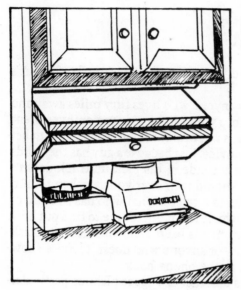

A fliptop garage keeps appliances out of sight, yet easy to reach.

After careful consideration, the designer will meet with you again to present you with his ideas and a bid. This proposal should include job description, price and terms of payment, approximate completion date, procedures for breaking the contract or making changes or corrections, cleanup responsibilities, and length and type of warranty.

As the construction date approaches, a few preliminary preparations will get things started quickly and smoothly. Take everything off kitchen walls and remove all decorations. Don't forget towel racks, hooks, wall hung appliances (or appliances attached to any cupboard that will be replaced). Remove the contents from all the cupboards and drawers. Take down curtains, Levolors, blinds, and all window treatment brackets.

If there is furniture in your kitchen (bar stools, TV, bookshelf, table and chairs, etc.), be sure to get it out of the way before the workmen begin.

Clear a spot in the basement, garage, carport, etc. where building materials and new appliances can be stored when they're delivered. Planning now will eliminate inconvenient disruptions later on.

If you're planning to do some (or all) of the work and designing yourself, get some good reference books. Two I frequently recommend are *The Motion-Minded Kitchen* by Sam Clark

(Houghton Mifflin Co.) and *Advanced Kitchens* by James E. Russel (Creative Homeowner Press). Time-Life Books and Sunset Books have a good planning and remodeling series, as well as *Family Circle's Remodeling Made Easy* magazine. All are helpful, easy to understand, and very visual guides.

APPLIANCES DESIGNED WITH YOUR ESCAPE IN MIND

Conquering time is our challenge today and manufacturers are answering the call with efficient, time-saving, and easy-to-care-for appliances. When considering the purchase of major appliances, get the most for your time and money by reviewing the following guidelines.

How much space is available? You may not have enough room for a double oven or a side-by-side refrigerator. Measure your spaces carefully.

What installation is required? Will you have to change or add different hookups at home—change from a gas stove to an electric model, add a water line for a refrigerator with an automatic icemaker or cold water dispenser, etc.?

Buy a good brand that has a reputation for durability. Check

A pop-up appliance shelf keeps your mixer out of sight, yet easy to use.

Consumer Reports and *Consumer's Research* at your local library. Look up the product in the Periodical Guide to see if other magazine articles have been written. Get good information from unbiased sources.

How long do you expect to use the product? List the features you want and arrange them in priority order. Look over owner's manuals before purchasing.

Shop around to discover the various models and styles available. If possible, talk to someone who owns a particular style you're considering. I was thinking seriously about purchasing a stove top advertised as almost revolutionary. I spoke to a friend who had one and she talked me out of it in a hurry. She found it extremely difficult to clean and she pointed out that the burners were so close together she couldn't put two large pans on the stove at the same time. I decided against the purchase and have been very happy with a much simpler model.

Remember that simplicity is the solution to a lot of problems. Some appliances nowadays will do everything but babysit. The more "gingerbread" you have tacked to your appliances, you increase proportionately the following: cost, chance of breakdown, repairs (costly in time and money), and cleaning around all the nooks and crannies.

Also in this same category are appliances that are built into

A pull-out corner base cupboard eliminates dead space and puts everything in full view.

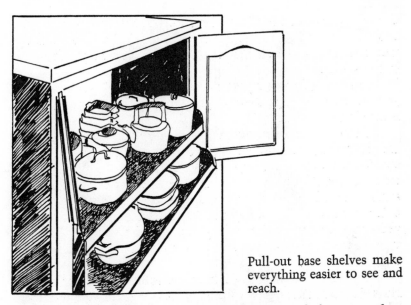

Pull-out base shelves make everything easier to see and reach.

the countertop. Aside from the above-mentioned objections they also limit your versatility and available counter space.

There are, however, some bona fide timesaving features that are worth the extra monetary investment. My favorites are: self-cleaning oven; snap-out electric heating elements on stove top; time-bake oven set (put food in the oven, set the timer and the oven starts and stops automatically); self-defrosting refrigerator/freezer with adjustable shelves; automatic ice-makers; built-in (as opposed to portable) dishwashers; continuous-feed garbage disposers; and textured appliance doors that disguise fingerprints.

Trash compactors are not included in this list of goodies. I have had more than one type of trash compactor and hated all of them. They need to be cleaned weekly, at least, and that alone can be a major undertaking. Frequently, too, a piece of sturdy trash will become lodged between the wastebasket and the plunger, making it impossible to open the compactor door. There may, of course, be millions of folks who couldn't live without their trash compactors, but I'm certainly not one of them. It's so much easier to use a tall plastic wastebasket with a plastic trash bag liner.

Basically, when weighing one model or feature against another, look for removable parts for easy cleaning, and adjustable shelves. Beware of carved, molded, or severely textured surfaces that will increase cleanup time.

Escape from the Kitchen

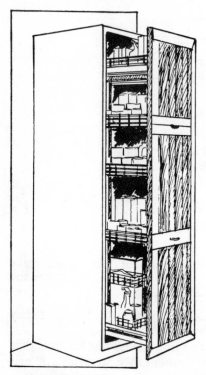

A pull-out pantry or chef's cupboard is an extra worth splurging on.

Read and understand the warranty. Buy the product from a reputable dealer who offers good, reliable service. At least, be sure that service centers for your particular appliance are readily available in your area. Also, ask about the appliance's expected lifespan.

When checking the cost of the appliance, ask if there are any other costs you're not aware of: delivery, installation, maintenance contracts, service charges, etc. Find out what the dealer's return policy is, should you be dissatisfied. Check to see if the appliance is safety-tested by a certifying agency (i.e. Underwriter's Laboratories, UL; Association of Home Appliance Manufacturers, AHAM; American Gas Association Blue Star).

Last, and certainly not least, when the appliance is delivered, take a few minutes to read the instruction manual. Using the appliance correctly will likely add years to its life. Keep the manual handy for periodic review until you're thoroughly familiar with the various functions of the product.

CUPBOARDS, COUNTERTOPS, FLOORS

You can save even more time by selecting easy care and efficient building materials.

Cupboards made from wood, metal, or plastic laminate are easier to clean if they have fewer trims, moldings, and grooves. They are more functional when shelves are adjustable and base cupboard shelves pull out.

Unless you're naturally neat and orderly, have doors installed on your cupboards. Open shelves and glass doors not only keep everything in full view, but can add to your cleaning time. Splashes, dust, grease splatters, etc. will settle on the shelves and their contents, or become obvious on glass doors. So think twice before choosing the "open" look.

Often shelves and drawer interiors are made from particle board type wood that has been oversprayed with a sealer. In time these surfaces swell and become rough to the touch. Also, cans, gadgets, pans, etc. mar the interior surface. The best alternative (albeit the most expensive) is to have shelves and drawers' interiors made from wood covered with plastic laminate. It's easy to clean, requires no shelf liner or painting, and looks good for years.

Some good built-in features are: slide-out garbage receptacles, bin drawers, spice cabinets or drawers, slide-out cutlery trays, and chef's cupboard. The illustrations in this chapter will give you many more ideas.

The main considerations when buying floor covering are easy care, comfort, price, durability, and beauty. Today, the runaway

A built-in spice rack installed in the front panel under the stove top provides one-motion storage.

best seller is the vinyl resilient floor. It's comfortable to stand on for long periods, it's easy to clean, and requires only occasional waxing or polishing (even no-wax floors); it's pretty, affordable, and does a good job of resisting grease and alkalis.

There are two basic types of vinyl: rotovinyl and inlaid. The rotovinyls have the pattern printed on the flooring. It's lighter in weight, which makes it easier for a do-it-yourselfer to install.

The inlaid vinyl's pattern is built up in layers made from vinyl granules that are fused together. This type of floor is more substantial (and more expensive) than a rotovinyl floor, and because of its sturdy construction it's harder for a nonprofessional to install.

Each floor type can be purchased with a vinyl or urethane no-wax finish. The vinyl resists stains better, but the urethane is tougher and keeps its shine better. For a high-traffic area like a kitchen, I would recommend an inlaid vinyl with a urethane finish. Armstrong's Solarian with Mirabond is an example.

Glazed brick and ceramic tile are other popular choices. They are extremely attractive, very durable, and keep their good looks for years. However, they're uncomfortable to stand on for long periods of time. Also, when a dish hits the floor you might as well get out the broom and dustpan.

Wood floors are very attractive. They're warm and durable and when covered with a penetrating seal are even moisture resistant. They can also be refinished (and need to be from time to time). Unless you're willing to pay a high maintenance price for the beauty of a wood floor, don't have one installed in your kitchen.

Kitchen carpeting is subject to much debate. You'll either love it or hate it with a vengeance. (I fall into the latter category, as does my counterpart, Don Aslett.) It's attractive, durable (and that's an understatement), and comfortable. But, things will spill, grease will splatter, and dogs and kids et al. will come in from the rain. Most of the folks I've spoken to who are kitchen carpet advocates have small families with older kids or no children.

Whatever your choice, select a covering that's awash with color. Golds and yellows magnify dirt and dark floors are especially hard to keep looking clean. Lighter shades (except stark white) are always preferred over dark.

When shopping for a countertop, look for the same features you'd want in a floor: easy care, durability, price, beauty, etc. Also, the same color guidelines apply (light colors are preferable to dark or white).

Plastic laminates are very popular (both smooth and textured). They are easy to clean and heat-resistant (not heat-proof), but they are subject to occasional cuts, stains, and burns. When purchasing this type of countertop, choose one with a molded backsplash for ease in cleaning.

Ceramic tile is pretty, durable, heatproof, and stands up to cutting and chopping. It wipes up easily, and individually damaged tiles can be replaced. I would recommend (when using ceramic tile anywhere) that you use a colored grout and always seal it. (Repeat the sealing procedure approximately once or twice a year.) On the downside, ceramic tile is noisy and dishes break more easily when dropped on the counter.

Wood or butcher block counters require special treatment (sanding, oiling) to keep them looking good. I prefer using a separate cutting board that can be stored in less than perfect condition under cover.

Synthetic marble looks like marble but has added advantages: it withstands heat, stains, and cracks. Although it scratches easily, mars can be "erased," in effect, by lightly sanding.

Metal counters or partial inserts are good for holding hot pans and bakeware. It does cut and scratch, however, so if you're leaning toward metal, choose a brushed satiny surfaced one that will camouflage the eventual wear and tear.

Marble is another possibility. It can crack and stain, though, and because it's enormously expensive it would be a good choice to use as a separate countertop or partial insert for pastry and candy making.

There are myriad choices for your countertops and floors. In this brief chapter, however, I've only attempted to discuss the most popular choices. For more information check with your kitchen planner, home center, department stores, builders, Yellow Pages, kitchen dealers, or the books I referred to earlier.

DESIGN INTERVENTION

- The garbage disposer should be installed in the sink closest to the mixing center.
- The dishwasher should be to the left of the sink if you're right-handed. Reverse it if you're left-handed.
- Some appliances come with removable colored panels so you

can change your decorating scheme without replacing the whole appliance.

- Appliances can be repainted by a professional who specializes in electrostatic painting. In fact, this process is perfect for any metal surface—bookcases, file cabinets, metal kitchen cabinets, etc.

- If your kitchen is tiny you will gain much-needed storage space by having ceiling-high cabinets installed.

- If your kitchen is open or visible from another room, be sure you coordinate the decorating schemes.

- An ordinary trellis, when painted to match your kitchen decor, can be attached to any vertical surface and used to hang gadgets, pans, etc. or to display collectibles. (Use S-hooks for hanging the equipment.)

- A decorative stepladder is handy as a plant stand when not being used for its intended purpose.

- Baskets are a great addition to any kitchen. Make an attractive grouping to hang on the wall; fill sitting or suspended baskets with magazines, plants, potatoes, apples, onions, pinecones, nuts, matchbook collection, cookie cutters, dried flowers, etc.

- For a clever and appealing way to get extra counter space, stand an antique ironing board in a kitchen corner. Even placed out of the way, this is a perfect spot to cool freshly baked goods, to serve a buffet, or to plan menus.

- Dispensers installed in the recesses between wall studs are handy for storing paper towels, bread, boxes of wraps, etc. This arrangement frees up counter and drawer space.

In the 17th century Henry Kett voiced this warning to all would-be builders and remodelers:

"Never build after you are five and forty; have five years' income in hand before you lay a brick; and always calculate the expense at double the estimate."

Though a kitchen renovation can be a David and Goliath confrontation, with the help of this chapter you, too, can fell the giant—even after you're forty-five!

SCULLERY MAID ESCAPES

MIDTOWN, USA
A three-state manhunt is under way for a self-styled scullery maid who cut her way out of her kitchen, where she was serving a fifty-year sentence for saying, "I do," at her wedding in 1978.

Iwanna B. Free escaped after serving eight years of her sentence, during which she cited irreconcilable differences with her kitchen.

Free, 32, apparently used one-motion storage in her carefully arranged kitchen work centers, where officers found dovetailed menu plans, an organized shopping list, and a full course meal bubbling in the oven.

She has eluded authorities for six months and officers admit that her escape plan is working. She has somehow managed to avoid the tactical pitfalls awaiting other convicts, authorities said.

Trail grows cold

Though bloodhounds have been following her scent, police confess that the trail has grown cold. Undercover agents have gathered only a meager amount of what appears to be circumstantial evidence. Found in Iwanna's freezer were two meatloaves, one deep-dish lasagne, and one enchilada supreme, and witnesses claim two of Free's children were seen emptying the dishwasher.

Officers admit the only hard piece of evidence they have to go on is Free's copy of the book, *Escape from the Kitchen*.

INDEX

P

Pan substitutes, 59
Pareto, Vilfredo, 1
Parties, holiday, 170-171
Party follow-up, 158-161
Party follow-up form, 160
Party method, 10
Party planner form, 155
Party planning, 153-156
Pile-It method, 9
Planning notebook, 142-143
Phone cord, 148
Prepared dishes in freezer
    form, 87
Preventive maintenance, 133-
    134
Prioritizing, 2-3, 9, 13-15, 31,
    41, 101, 102

R

Recipes, 123-132
Recipes, collecting, 86, 87-89
Recipes, selecting, 82-83
Refrigerator, 71, 72
Refrigerator center, 28-29, 30-
    32
Remodeling, 179-184

S

Serving center, 27-28, 30-32,
    70-71
Shelf storage, 53-54, 66-67
Shopping list form, 100
Sink center, 22-23, 30-32, 35
Spice storage, 44, 61-64
Storage at the point of first
    use, 12
Storage principles, 12-17
Store guide chart, 102
Store guide form, 103

T

Tidbit method, 9
Time Power, 4
Timetable for organizing, 47
Tool box, 146-147
Toss it, move it method, 9

W

Woman's Day magazine, 69
Work centers, 2, 11-12, 21-29,
    30-32, 38-41

Other Books by Deniece Schofield

Confessions of an Organized Housewife—Specific ideas for organizing every aspect of home life. 214 pages, $6.95, paper

Confessions of a Happily Organized Family—Ways to get your family working together to establish a comfortable sense of order in your home. 246 pages, $7.95, paper

Other "Home Care" Books from Writer's Digest Books

Make Your House Do the Housework, by Don Aslett, $9.95, paper
Who Says It's a Woman's Job to Clean?, by Don Aslett, $5.95, paper
Is There Life After Housework?, by Don Aslett, $7.95, paper
Clutter's Last Stand, by Don Aslett, $8.95, paper
Do I Dust or Vacuum First?, by Don Aslett, $6.95, paper
How to Get Organized When You Don't Have the Time, by Stephanie Culp, $9.95, paper
It's Here . . . Somewhere!, by Alice Fulton & Pauline Hatch, $6.95, paper
Teach Me Mommy: A Preschool Home Learning Guide, by Jill Dunford, $11.95, paper

Coupon:

- -

YES! Please send me the following books:
_____ (1143) Confessions of an Organized Housewife, $6.95
_____ (1145) Confessions of a Happily Organized Family, $7.95
_____ (1242) Escape from the Kitchen, $7.95

_____

_____

_____

(Please add $2.00 postage & handling for one book, 50¢ for each additional book. Ohio residents add 5½% sales tax.)
☐ Payment enclosed ☐ Please charge my: ☐ Visa ☐ MasterCard
　Acct. # _____ Exp. Date _____
　Signature _____
Name _____
Address _____
City _____ State _____ Zip _____

Send to: WRITER'S DIGEST BOOKS, 9933 Alliance Road, Cincinnati, OH 45242

- -

For information on organizational products and seminars, write to:
　Deniece Schofield
　P.O. Box 492
　Bountiful, UT 84010
　(Prices subject to change without notice.)

2212